ENTER THE WATER
COME TO THE TABLE

ENTER THE WATER
COME TO THE TABLE

Baptism and the Lord's Supper
in Scripture's Story of New Creation

JOHN MARK HICKS

Abilene Christian University Press

Enter the Water, Come to the Table

Baptism and the Lord's Supper in Scripture's Story of New Creation

ACU
PRESS

Copyright 2014 by John Mark Hicks

ISBN 978-0-89112-483-2

Printed in the United States of America

Scripture quotations, unless otherwise noted, are from the New Revised Standard
Version Bible, copyright 1989, Division of Christian Education of the National Council of
the Churches of Christ in the United States of America. Used by permission. All rights
reserved.

Cover design by Rick Gibson
Interior text design by Sandy Armstrong, Strong Design

For information contact:
Abilene Christian University Press
1626 Campus Court
Abilene, Texas 79601

1-877-816-4455 toll free
www.acupressbooks.com

14 15 16 17 18 19 / 7 6 5 4 3 2 1

Throughout thirty-two years of teaching in
higher education among Churches of Christ,
I have been *informed* and *inspired*
by those who have been in my classes.
Thank you!

Acknowledgements

Mike Cope, director of the Pepperdine University Bible Lectures, was the first to suggest that I write something that would complement the 2014 lectures. Then, Leonard Allen, of Abilene Christian University Press, invited me to publish once again on baptism and the Lord's supper. I am grateful for their confidence and the opportunities they have given me. I would not have written this new material without their initiative and encouragement.

Throughout the process my wife, Jennifer, and my sister-in-law, Melanie Crotty, have helped me in many ways. They reviewed the manuscript, and they provided the space and support I needed to finish the work. I am grateful for their assistance.

I am also grateful for the many contexts in which so many have shaped my thinking in classes, blogs, emails, congregations, and seminars. There are far too many to mention here, but every word, dialogue, and encounter has impacted and sharpened my understanding.

Most of the material in this book is new, but some of it draws heavily from my published works or blogs at johnmark-hicks.com. From published works, the most significant are *Come to the Table* (Leafwood Publishers, 2008); *Down in the River to Pray* with Greg Taylor, rev. ed. (Leafwood Publishers, 2010); "Eschatological Table" in *Evangelicalism and the Stone-Campbell Movement, Vol. 2* (ACU Press, 2006); "Safe, to Lost, to Saved?" *Christian Standard* (August 2010), 582; and "A Sacramental Journey: A Christian-Theological Reading of Exodus," *Leaven* 21.2 (2013), 60-64.

I deeply appreciate how readers have received my previous writings on baptism and the Lord's supper, and I hope that this new offering will deepen our appreciation and further enrich our understanding of God's gifts.

Soli Deo Gloria.

Table of Contents

SACRAMENTAL THEOLOGY?

I recognize that "sacramental theology" carries negative baggage for many. I could avoid this language, but there are reasons to emphasize the *sacramental* character of baptism, Lord's supper and—I would add—the assembly.[1]

If "sacrament" means some kind of ritualistic power rooted in institutionalism or clerical authority, then I'm not interested. If "sacrament" has overtones of "magical powers" or "superstition," I'm not interested in that either. If "sacrament" entails that faith is unnecessary or that the ritualistic act itself (in terms of its own power) imparts grace, then I'm certainly not interested. However, "sacrament" does not necessarily mean any of those things. Wherever those ideas are

11

present—if they are present—they are layers placed on top of the central idea of sacramental theology.

That central idea is: *God acts through appointed means to impart grace, assurance, and hope.* I prefer "sacrament" to "ordinance" precisely because I want to emphasize that *God works* through these means.

Popular Christianity is often anthropocentric (human-centered) in its approach to baptism, Lord's supper, and the assembly. The "ordinances" are often regarded as mere acts of human obedience. They are primarily, if not exclusively, something *we do.* Stressing their "sacramental" nature, however, need not undermine their function as "ordinances." But stressing it moves us toward a more theocentric understanding as we recognize them as divine acts of grace.

How might we think about these Christian "ordinances" as "sacraments"? Instead of polarizing the two designations, just perhaps *together* they embrace the fullness of what God has invested in baptism, the Lord's supper, and the assembly.

Definition of a Sacrament

Sacramentum, the original Latin word, is sometimes translated "pledge" and at other times "mystery." Both meanings have advocates, and both are appropriate. However, as Calvin argued in his *Institutes of Christian Religion* (IV.xiv.13), the mystery of the sacrament is more fundamental than its pledging function. The sacraments are more than simple "church ordinances." Their pledging function is significant *because* they are divine mysteries. The power of the sacrament is God's work, which we embrace through faith.

When viewed primarily or solely as human pledge, our "sacramental" theology is anthropocentric because it prioritizes what *we do*—we pledge allegiance, we testify to God's grace, we obey, we remember, we gather, etc. But sacrament as mystery is theocentric because it emphasizes what God does—God acts through the sacraments by the Spirit through faith. Both perspectives are important, but divine action grounds and gives meaning to our obedience. The sacraments are concrete moments in time and space that not only signify the gospel and bear witness to the gospel, but they are also means through which God acts to communicate grace to believers.

Sacraments, as I understand them, are (1) *material* realities that (2) *represent* the reality of the gospel, that is, they are concrete signs that point beyond themselves to the work of God in Christ. But they do more than point; they are (3) *means of grace* that participate in the reality to which they point and are joined to that reality by the promise of God's Word. This experience is (4) *eschatological* as we participate in the present-yet-future reality of the kingdom of God. We are raised with Christ through baptism, eat with Jesus at the Messianic banquet, and assemble around the throne of God. The power of this sacramental moment, however, is not contained in the sign itself but (5) is effected *by the Spirit* who mediates the presence of God through the sacrament as (6) we receive what God gives *through faith*. The ground of God's gracious acts in the sacraments is the (7) *reconciling work of Christ* through his incarnation, ministry, death, resurrection, and ascension.

The sacraments are a human witness to the grace of God as well as a human pledge of allegiance to the story of God in Jesus. They are also, however, divine pledges of assurance and means by which God encounters, communes with, and transforms believers into the image of Christ.

Sacramental Foundations

The sacraments are present throughout redemptive history. God's story is a sacramental journey, analogous to a five-act drama.

Act One: Creation. Some reject sacramental mystery because it involves material objects. Nothing external or physical, it is said, can mediate the spiritual. Ultimately, however, this denies the goodness of creation. The creation is God's temple. God rested in the creation and was present through the tree of life, walking in the garden, and sharing life with humanity. Materiality does not hinder communion with God but mediates it. We experience something of this through nature walks, watching falling snow, sitting on cliffs overlooking the Pacific, or watching a beautiful sunset. We feel God's presence in such moments.

Act Two: Israel. While some dismiss the "externals" and "ceremonies" of Israel, these were sacramental occasions of God's presence within Israel. The temple, for example, was no mere symbol of divine presence, but was truly God's communing presence though it, of course, could not contain the fullness of God. Circumcision sealed the promise of God, their sacrifices mediated forgiveness and their meals were occasions for rejoicing before the Lord, and their assemblies "saw" God. Though these ceremonies were fulfilled in Christ, they were nevertheless authentic experiences of divine presence.

Act Three: Christ. The theological root of sacramental theology is Christ, the sacrament of God. The incarnation sanctified creation—God became flesh and flesh mediated God's presence to the world. God in the flesh affirms materiality. The fullness of God dwelt in the physical body of Jesus. To polarize materiality and spirituality is to undermine the incarnation where the material and spiritual are united in the person of Jesus. The sacraments draw their meaning, power, and efficacy from the union of God and creation in the incarnation. They are fundamentally Christological rather than ecclesiological since Jesus himself is sacrament. If flesh and deity are united in Jesus, God can unite materiality and grace in baptism, the Lord's supper, and the assembly. Indeed, the latter is grounded in the former.

Moreover, Jesus himself, as the Incarnate God, participated in Israel's sacramental journey. He was baptized with Israel, assembled with Israel in its festive celebrations (Sabbaths, Passovers, Feast of Tabernacles, etc.), and ate at those tables. Jesus embraced Israel's sacraments. More than that, he gave them new meaning, depth, and significance. Jesus did not discontinue the sacramental journey. On the contrary, he kicked it up a notch.

Act Four: Church. As the "second incarnation" of Jesus in the world, the church is itself a sacramental reality. The church is the body of Christ, and God dwells in the bodies of believers through the Spirit of God. We—finite, embodied people—are the habitation of God. This is no figure of speech. We are sacramental beings; we live each moment as divine dwelling places.

Act Five: Eschaton. While the church is flawed by its own sin, she is the body of Christ and remains an authentic sacrament of God's presence. This eschatological community of God will enjoy entire sanctification in both body and soul in the new heaven and new earth. The Spirit of God will transform our bodies from mortality to immortality. We will live on the new heaven and new earth in spiritual bodies, that is, material bodies animated by the Spirit of God. Our immortal bodies will be sacramental dwelling places of God's Spirit, and God will fully rest in the new creation.

This is God's overarching, sacramental story; the sacraments exist as God's gifts to the church. Through them we taste the future that assures and confirms our faith in the present. In the sacraments the future becomes present. That future is the new creation, begun in the resurrection of Jesus and given to us in the sacraments. The sacraments mark our journey of faith from creation to new creation.

High Drama in Community: Baptism, the Lord's Supper, and Assembly

Baptism, the Lord's supper, and assembly are dramatic rehearsals of the story through which God renews communion, empowers transformation, and realizes the future. By faith the community participates in this story through water, food and drink, and gathering in the power of the Spirit.

These gospel "ordinances" (or sacraments) have ordinarily (though with some variation) been construed in this manner: (1) Baptism is a means of grace for justification through participation in the death and resurrection of Jesus, (2) the Lord's supper is a means of grace for sanctification through remembrance of and communion with the death of Christ, and (3) the Lord's day is a means of grace for communal worship through celebration of the resurrection (new creation). In this sense, they not only bear witness to the gospel as "ordinances," but they are also sacramental means through which believers experience the grace of the gospel in the Spirit. In other words, these gospel symbols mediate the presence of Christ to his community. *They are both ordinances and sacraments!*

They are not substitutes for discipleship or transformation but rather moments of divine-human encounter through which we are moved along the path of discipleship toward entire sanctification. This kind of sacramentalism is not popular. Many empty all sacramental imagination from these ordinances. Baptism becomes either a mere symbol or a test of loyalty. The Lord's supper becomes an anthropocentric form of individualistic piety. Assembly becomes either a legal test of faithfulness or a mere occasion for mutual encouragement that is susceptible to pragmatic consumerism.

In *Come to the Table*, I suggested that the Lord's Supper is an authentic communion with God through Christ in the power of the Spirit. Additionally, in *Down in the River to Pray*, Greg Taylor and I suggested that baptism is a means of grace through which we encounter the saving act of God in Christ through his death and resurrection. Further, in *A Gathered People*, Bobby Valentine, Johnny Melton and I suggested that assembly, wherever and whenever a community of Christ-followers gather to seek God's face, participates in the eschatological assembly because the Spirit ushers us into the heavenly

Jerusalem where we share the future with all the saints gathered around the world and spread throughout time. Baptism, the Lord's supper, and assembly are moments of communion, participation, and encounter.

The Plan of the Book

This book explores the meaning and practice of baptism and the Lord's supper through the lens of Scripture's movement from creation to new creation. Rooting this sacramental journey in the exodus of Israel, Jesus inaugurated a new exodus from old creation into new creation. Jesus' own baptism and his table practice embodied the kingdom of God in his ministry.

The sacraments bind us to God's story from creation to new creation. We are united with Israel's exodus from bondage, their journey through the wilderness, and their entrance into their promised inheritance. We are united with Jesus as he is immersed in the Jordan, prays in the wilderness, feasts at the tables, dies on the cross, and ascends into the heavenlies in a resurrected body. We are united with the church throughout the world and into the future. We embrace the future of God's creation in Christ and experience the newness of redeemed creation as we share the resurrection of Jesus in our baptism, are nourished by the living Christ through the supper, and are brought before the throne of God in assembly. The story of God in Scripture becomes our story through the sacraments, and through the sacraments we remember, embrace, experience, and commit ourselves to the story of God.

CREATION (Genesis 1-2)

When God began to create the heavens and the earth, "the earth was a formless void and darkness covered the face of the deep" as the Spirit of God hovered "over the face of the waters." God first created this "formless void" from nothing, but then began to work with this dark uninhabitable wasteland, a chaotic emptiness enveloped in darkness. The imagery is almost sinister. The "waters" are ominous; the earth was a threatening, uninhabitable sphere.

God, however, took this "formless void" and through loving power created a good, habitable home where God and humanity might dwell together. God constructed a cosmic temple in which to dwell and created humanity to serve as royal priests. Humanity was invited to partner with God in caring for and developing the creation. Out of the murky chaos of the "formless void" God made the heavens and earth as a "good" habitation for both God and humanity, a cosmic temple where God dwelt with and loved humanity.

The creation story suggests a baptismal picture. The dark and disordered world was submerged under water. The "deep" had swallowed the earth. Through God's creative breath, God's Spirit, the earth emerged from the waters as a habitable world. The first day of creation separated light from darkness, or perhaps better, injected light into the dark chaos. The second day separated "waters from the waters" in order to provide space for the sky within the waters. The third day separated the "waters under the sky" from "dry land." The first three days of creation poetically describe how God brought a new heavens and earth out of the dark chaotic waters! New life then appeared in the remaining three days of creation. *The cosmos arose from a watery grave!*

The creation story also suggests a eucharistic picture of food and drink. Eden, the sanctuary of God's temple, was a garden planted "in the east" where the sun rises. A river arising from the heart of the garden watered Eden. The river became four rivers that would water "the whole face of the ground." Rather than threatening chaos, this water gave life to the earth. These were streams of living water. Through this irrigation, God brought forth life from the ground. Vegetation gave the earth its color. Every tree was pleasing to the eye and "good for food," including the "tree of life" which was in the middle of the garden. Food and drink were integral to Eden.

They were part of the goodness of creation. *Food and drink were life-giving gifts!*

God placed humanity in that life-giving and life-affirming sanctuary. God created a community—male and female—to inhabit the garden. Together they pursued their missional vocation to fill the earth, partner with God in subduing the remaining chaos within creation, and share the divine task of shepherding the creation. Humanity—male and female—represented God within the creation as they served and protected the earth. Adam and Eve were God's royal priests within the cosmic temple as they ate and drank in the presence of God.

Life in Eden was thoroughly sacramental. The heavens and earth emerged from a watery chaos as a new creation. Eden was planted and watered by God. Every breath was communion with God. Every meal and drink was enjoyed in God's presence. Humanity lived in God's temple as junior partners in the dynamic adventure that would produce the future.

Created life was *baptismal* in origin and *eucharistic* in character. Rather than simply *homo sapiens*, they were more fundamentally *homo liturgicus*, that is, they lived, breathed, and moved within God's life and enjoyed the created order as God's good gift. Everything about human life was sacramental since it breathed the presence of God. Every aspect of life was sacred and good. It was full of joy, and it anticipated a future filled with new delights.

But chaos still lurked. The waters, though bounded, still existed. Darkness, though sprinkled with the lights of the night, was yet present. Even in Eden a serpent appeared to probe, question, and tempt humanity. Indeed, the serpent diverted humanity from its divine mission. Rather then representing God and enjoying the vocation God gave them, people—as Genesis 3-11 tells us—pursued their own agenda and sought to make a name for themselves. From the blood of Abel to the Tower of Babel humanity tumbled into darkness and chaos, and God's good creation was subjected to futility. The sacramental nature of life was obscured as food and drink became tears and lament, and the waters flooded the earth.

The once new creation had aged as darkness dimmed the good light of God. Violence and death shattered the peace of Eden. Now creation groaned for liberation; it groaned for renewal.

Renewal is a sacramental journey.

Chapter 1

ISRAEL:
From Exodus to Sinai

Human history tumbled into the abyss of violence and self-aggran-dizing power. From the blood of Abel to the arrogant reach for reputation at Babel, we degenerated into a chaotic mass that grieved the heart of God. Rather than annihilating the creation, however, God chose to redeem it. The descendants of Abraham, God promised, would bless all nations and inherit the earth.

Israel's national history, promised in Abraham, begins with the exodus. The mighty acts of God created and sustained Israel in their journey from Egypt to Canaan. The exodus story created, identified, and guided Israel as Yahweh's elect people. The confluence of themes that constitute this identity provides the basic lens through which Israel knows itself and through which the church identifies with Israel. These themes—creation, redemption, and divine presence—shape the life of Israel and subsequently the church.

Sacramental themes appear in the book of Exodus. They underscore the divine grace mediated by creation (water, food, cloud, fire). Israel's sacramental experience encounters a gracious God and typifies the church's own experience of that same God. Early Christians read the Exodus narrative as their own. That narrative was rehearsed in both word and ritual as the exodus found its climactic fulfillment in Christ. Early Christians saw their own baptism, eating and drinking at a table, and worship assemblies in Israel's redemption.

The book of Exodus is structured in three theological-geographical moves.[1] The first movement is from slavery to liberation (Exod. 1:1-15:21), the second from wilderness to Sinai (Exod. 15:22-24:18), and the third from Sinai to tabernacle (Exod. 25-40). Each of these has a sacramental climax. Israel is baptized in the sea and cloud, eats with God on Sinai, and enjoys God's descent upon the tabernacle to dwell within Israel.

Enter the Water: Baptized in the Cloud and Sea

The crossing of the sea marks Israel's liberation from Egyptian slavery, and the waters—the very symbol of chaos—defeat the hostile powers that arrayed themselves against God's people. Water separated life from death.

The Exodus Story

As the story opens in Exodus, Israel is enslaved in Egypt. The people "groaned under their slavery and cried out." Though

God appears absent, God heard their cry and remembered the covenant with Abraham (Exod. 2:23-24). Responding, God appeared to Moses and sent him to Egypt. God undermined Egyptian confidence in their own deities through a form of uncreation (the reversal of creation) in the ten plagues. Chaos filled the good creation as God afflicted Egypt for the sake of liberating Israel.

Though Pharaoh released Israel in the face of divine uncreation, he soon pursued her. Fear raged through Israel, but Moses assured her. At the edge of the sea God moved between the Egyptians and Israel. The "cloud was there with the darkness," that is, God was present in the night to protect Israel from the Egyptians. Yahweh was "in the pillar of fire and the cloud" (Exod. 14:19, 24). The cloud and the fire functioned sacramentally. Israel recognized this point and celebrated it in their liturgies (Pss. 78:14; 99:7; 105:38-39).

The "waters" figure prominently in the narrative at this point. The "waters" echo the creation account (Gen. 1:2, 6-7, 9-10). They were part of the primordial chaos. God "separated the waters" to make space for the earth. God "gathered" the "waters" into a single place so that dry land might emerge. The "waters" are the presence of chaos within the creation.

The "waters" also echo the flood narrative (Gen. 6:17; 7:6-7, 10, 24; 8:1-3; 9:15). The "flood of waters" was released upon the earth to destroy it. When the "waters gradually receded from the earth," a new creation emerged along with the divine promise that the "waters" would never again "destroy all flesh." God cleansed the earth through the "waters."

Early Christians saw a parallel between their baptism and the Noahic flood (1 Pet. 3:20-21). The eight persons who found refuge in the ark from the destructive floodwaters were, in fact, "saved through water," and this prefigures how Christians are also saved through water. Baptism, like the flood, is a means by which God rescues. Just as God saved Noah through cleansing the old world with water, so God saves us by putting to death our old lives and giving new life through baptism. In the Noahic flood, water cleansed the old world. Baptism cleanses our old lives. To use a Pauline metaphor, baptismal water drowns the old person, buries it, and then renews it. Just as Noah passed through the waters into a new world, so we pass through baptism into a new creation. Though chaotic "waters" often threaten life, God redeems through them.

Israel, at the edge of the sea, faced the destructive, chaotic "waters." On the one hand, Israel faced the chaotic darkness of destruction from the Egyptian army. On the other hand, they faced the overwhelming presence of the "waters." They seemed trapped between hostile forces. In this moment, Yahweh directs Israel to move forward *through* the waters.

What follows is the most memorable and most significant moment in the history of Israel. Yahweh confronts the chaos, just as God did at creation. A wind, like the Spirit in creation, blew over the sea and "the waters were divided" so that "dry land" appeared. The "waters" were like a "wall" on "their right and on their left." They loomed over Israel like impending chaos. Israel, trusting in Yahweh, "walked on dry ground through the sea." On that day, Yahweh "saved Israel."

Israel "saw the great power of the Lord" and "believed in the Lord and in his servant Moses" (Exod. 14:21, 22, 29-31).

This is creation language. The *ruach* (Spirit, breath, wind) of God hovered over the waters in Genesis 1, and God brought forth dry land. Similarly, through the emergence of dry land in the midst of the waters a new world opens up for Israel. They leave their old world behind and walk toward a new one, their inheritance in the land promised to Abraham. They escaped the chaos of the "waters" because God divided the "waters," just as in the beginning. Liberated from slavery, a new identity filled with hope and promise awaited Israel. The exodus was new creation.

Early Christians connected the exodus with their own baptism. Israel was "baptized into Moses in the cloud and in the sea" (1 Cor. 10:2). Israel was given a new identity when they passed through the waters. In the same way, believers in Christ receive a new identity when they pass through the waters into a new life. God creates anew through baptism. Israel and the church share sacramental meaning—God has acted through the waters to save each from chaotic darkness.

Water Rituals in Israel

While the "waters" represent chaos, they also function as a cleansing agent. The flood cleansed the earth. Israel practiced water rituals—immersions—for the purpose of cleansing. The waters judged the old life (whatever the contagion) and washed them clean.

One of the foundational principles of Christianity is the "instruction about baptisms" (Heb. 6:2). The plural may seem rather curious, but first-century readers were well aware of the pervasive character of immersion rituals in first-century Judaism. They also knew the baptismal regulations in Leviticus 15 (Heb. 9:10; "various *baptismois*"). The preacher invited readers to discern the difference between Christian baptism, which lies at the foundation of Christian faith and repentance, and the baptisms of the Levitical order that could "not perfect the conscience of the worshiper" (Heb. 9:9). The Levitical baptisms were shadows of Christian baptism.

Two kinds of immersions are prescribed in the Torah. *First, ritual immersions prepared priests for holy service in the sanctuary.* On the Day of Atonement the high priest bathed before putting on sacred garments and after removing them (Lev. 16:4, 24). These immersions separated the individuals from the impurities of life. They were not so much a moral purification as they set the priests apart for their holy tasks. They were cleansed or consecrated through washing before they stood in God's holy presence on behalf of the people.

Hebrews 10:22 applies this priestly typology to Christian experience. Just as priests drew near to God in their liturgical service, so believers "draw near" to God in theirs (cf. Lev. 9:5-7; Heb. 7:25; 10:1). Just as the high priest approached God through the curtain of the Holy of Holies, we approach God through the flesh of Christ who is our high priest. We draw near to God in full assurance with sincere hearts.

More to the point, just as the high priest immersed himself before entering the Holy of Holies, so our bodies are washed before we draw near to God. Hebrews 10:22 uses the identical language of Leviticus: wash, body, and water (cf.

Lev. 16:4, 23, 26, 28). Washing precedes entrance; Christian immersion, however, is no mere external ritual. Rather, the heart is also sprinkled with blood just as the body is washed with water. Those who approach God to enter the heavenly Holy of Holies are sprinkled with the blood of Jesus and washed with pure water.

Second, ritual immersions were important for ritual purity in cases of physical defilement. After exposure to diseases, everyone bathed for ceremonial purity (Lev. 14:8-9). After bodily discharges, everyone bathed (Lev. 15:5-11, 13, 16, 18, 21-22, 27). After eating something killed by wild animals, everyone bathed (Lev. 17:15). After touching anything unclean, everyone bathed (Lev. 22:6).

Levitical washings were external regulations that could not cleanse the conscience (Heb. 9:9). They were concerned with ritual purity and physical defilement, not with moral purification. This is a difference between Levitical baptisms and Christian baptism. The difference is not the washing itself, but the sacrifice that grounds them (Heb. 9:13-14; 10:2-4, 11-12, 19-22). The blood sprinkled upon the heart in the context of Christian baptism is the blood of Jesus, which is able to cleanse the conscience where the blood of animals could not.

Ultimately, both forms of ritual washing, whether priestly or ritual purity, served a more fundamental purpose. They both represented some kind of cleansing which prepared the worshipper to draw near to God. Ritual impurity hindered their approach to God. The water rituals cleansed them so that they might enter God's presence. This, too, is a function of Christian baptism. We pass through the waters into God's holy presence.

Come to the Table: Eating with God

Israel's encounter with God at Sinai, called the "day of the assembly" (Deut. 9:10; 10:4; 18:16), shaped the liturgical meaning of Israel's tables. Whenever they consumed a sacrificial meal, they ate in God's presence.

Encountering God at Sinai

After their baptism in the sea and cloud, God led Israel "into the wilderness" (Exod. 15:22). Though Israel complained about their thirst and hunger, Yahweh nevertheless provided water and manna. God transformed the desert into new life for newborn Israel. Where there were only rocks and shrubs, God gave the water of life and the bread of heaven. This is the promise of new creation—of new life—in the midst of barrenness. This itself has sacramental meaning. Their food and drink in the wilderness was "spiritual," drawn from Christ himself (1 Cor. 10:2-4).

Exodus 15:22-24:18 moves Israel from the sea through the wilderness to "the mountain of God" at Sinai where the "glory" of Yahweh "dwelt" (Exod. 24:13, 16). Exodus 15:17 celebrates this movement in the conclusion of Israel's victory song:

> You brought them in and planted them on the
> mountain of your own possession,
> the place, O LORD, that you made your abode,

the sanctuary, O LORD, that your hands have
established.

The wilderness led Israel to God's mountain. The pillar of
cloud and fire led Israel to God's "sanctuary."

In Exodus 19-24, God covenants with Israel. Yahweh
invited Israel into a covenant relationship and they accepted
(Exod. 19:3-8). Then God showed up—Sinai was covered with
a "thick cloud" as God came to dwell on the mountain in
order to "meet" Israel (Exod. 19:9, 16-17). But the people were
warned that they must not presume upon God's invitation
and "break through to the Lord" since God's holiness would
"break out against them" (Exod. 19:21-22). The people must
learn the way of the covenant, commit to it, and approach
God through divine grace rather than rushing presumptu-
ously into God's presence. The covenant is summarized in the
Decalogue (Exod. 20:1-17) and then elaborated in the "book of
the covenant" (Exod. 21-23). Only then is the covenant ratified
through bloody sacrifices and a meal (Exod. 24:1-11).

Mirroring Exodus 19 as a second ratification, Israel covenants with God through burnt offerings and fellowship offerings in Exodus 24:1-11. An altar and a table stand at the heart
of this passage. The altar and its sacrifices are the ground upon
which Moses and the elders are invited into the presence of
God to eat and drink at a table. Having sprinkled the "blood of
the covenant" on the people, the representatives of Israel climb
Sinai to meet God. There the leaders of Israel eat and drink in
God's presence. Astonishingly, Exodus 24:11 succinctly but
profoundly reports: "they saw God, and they ate and drank."

However, the God of Israel is a holy God whom sinful humans cannot approach. But God established communion with Israel through the altar. To reinforce the significance of this moment, the text *again* states that they "saw God" (Exod. 33:20). Because of the sacrifices, they experienced God without being consumed. They communed with God at the table. God became the God of Israel through covenant, and this covenant was celebrated with a meal. The altar led to a table. At the table they ate and drank in God's presence.

This is a revolutionary moment. This eating and drinking with God on the holy mountain became the fundamental truth of Israel's sacrificial meals. When Israel ate and drank— fellowship meals—they did so "before the LORD" (Deut. 27:7). It was as if they were eating and drinking in the Holy Place itself that is "before the LORD" (Exod. 28:35). That Israel "saw" God is the foundational theology for standing, eating, or rejoicing "before the LORD" (cf. Exod. 27:21; 28:12, 29, 35, 38; 29:11, 23-26, 42; 30:8, 16; 34:34; 40:23, 25). Sacrificial meals were sacramental meals "before the LORD." In a real sense all subsequent meals in Israel re-present this moment when Israel "saw God" at the table on God's holy mountain.

The sacramental meal in the church recalls that moment. At the Last Supper Jesus described the wine of the Passover as the "blood of the covenant" (Matt. 26:27), a clear allusion to Exodus 24:8. The blood is the enactment of the covenant. The blood is poured out at the altar. The cross is the Christian altar, but the Lord's supper is the Christian table. Just as a table follows the altar in Exodus 24, so the table of the Lord follows the cross of Christ. Because the altar grounds our forgiveness and reconciliation, we are able to commune with God at the table.

Israel's Fellowship Meals

When stressing the significance of the Lord's table for Christian living, Paul suggested that Israel's meals were a model for the Christian table. "Consider the people of Israel," he wrote (1 Cor. 10:18), "are not those who eat the sacrifices partners in the altar?" This parallel suggests that we should pay careful attention to what happened at Israel's meals. [2]

Worshippers immersed themselves in water before night-fall the day before the ritual. Before they entered the temple, they immersed themselves again in one of the Jewish "baptistries" provided at the foot of the Temple Mount. Worshippers brought an animal and laid their hands on it to declare their intention. They might dedicate the sacrifice as a thanksgiving for some blessing or make a vow before the Lord (Lev. 7:12, 16). The sacrifice also included a bread offering with yeast (Lev. 7:12-13; thus, leavened bread) as well as a drink offering (Ps. 116:13-17). The sacrifice, therefore, was a meal with meat, bread, and drink (Num. 6:17; 15:1-12).

Worshippers killed the animals by slitting their throats. The priests would catch the blood in bowls and pour them around the altar. The animals were then butchered in the temple precincts. The fat was burned on the altar as "a food-offering" since "all fat is the LORD's" (Lev. 3:11, 16-17). The worshippers took the breasts and waved them before the Lord as a gift to God and then gave the breasts and right thighs to the priests. The priests shared this with their families (Lev. 7:14).

The worshippers took the remainder home for a festive meal with family and friends.

The communal dimension of the meal is apparent. The meal involves God, the priests, and the worshippers (including their family and friends). The community participates in the meal. God is a participant as well. The meal displays the relational dimensions of Israel's faith. No one eats alone. Israel eats as a community in fellowship with God and each other.

The fellowship meal appears regularly in the pages of the Hebrew Bible:

- It is shared at the ratification of the Mosaic covenant (Exod. 24:5).
- It inaugurates the priesthood (Lev. 9:4, 18, 22).
- It is part of every major festival, including Passover, Pentecost, and Tabernacles (Num. 29:39).
- It was part of the covenant renewal at Shechem (Deut. 27:7; Josh. 8:31).
- Israel celebrated the arrival of the ark of the covenant into Jerusalem by eating fellowship offerings (2 Sam. 6:17; 1 Chron. 16:1-2).
- Fellowship offerings were eaten at the dedication of the temple (2 Chron. 7:7).
- They were also part of Hezekiah's two-week Passover celebration (2 Chron. 29:35; 30:22).
- The thanksgiving offering is also prominent in the Psalms (cf. Pss. 50:14, 23; 56:12-13; 107:22; 116:12-17).

These sacrifices were a daily occurrence at the temple.

Several features characterize the fellowship meals of Israel. *First, it is a moment of communion between God and the community.* God is present; it is eaten before the Lord as if God sits at the table with the worshipper. Thus, worshippers eat with assurance, thanksgiving, and confidence.

Second, it is a communal act among the covenant people of God. It is a shared offering—shared with God, the priests, and the community (friends and family). Worshippers shared the meal with others. God never intended humans to eat alone.

Third, it is characterized by joy and gratitude. The fellowship offering is a festive occasion. It is a time of celebration, dedication, and renewal. "Days of rejoicing" characterized all Israel's festivals (Num. 10:10).

Yahweh Dwells With Israel

In Exodus 25-40 the narrative stalls. The people do not move; they remain at Sinai. Instead, the text details the plans for (Exod. 25-31) and the building of (Exod. 35-40) the tabernacle. The golden calf episode (Exod. 32-34) occupies the center of the tabernacle story. The preparation and building of the tabernacle anticipates God's coming. Even the drama of the golden calf results in God's renewed promise to dwell with Israel (Exod. 33:12-17). The Exodus narrative climaxes when God descends to dwell among the chosen people (Exod. 40:35). Rather than the people, this time God moves from Sinai to the tabernacle.

This divine movement from Sinai to tabernacle, as Terence Fretheim notes, is a movement from "*occasional* appearances of God" on Sinai to "the *ongoing* presence of God" in the tabernacle.[3] This closes the distance between God and Israel. No longer is God "over there" or even "up there" but rather God is "here"—God is present among them. Israel now comes "before the LORD" because God is sacramentally present in the tabernacle.

One way to see this point is to note the use of the verb "dwell" in the story. The Hebrew term (*shekan* from which the word *shekinah* is formed) is used five times in this narrative (Exod. 24:16; 25:8; 29:45-46; 40:35). At the beginning of the narrative the "glory of the Lord dwelt on Mt. Sinai." But by the end of the narrative "the cloud" will "settle" (literally, dwell) on the "tent of meeting" as the "glory of the LORD filled the tabernacle." The tabernacle becomes God's sanctuary where God dwells "in their midst." This movement from Sinai to tabernacle is the realization of the covenantal promise: "I will dwell among the people of Israel and will be their God." Indeed, this is the significance of the exodus itself. God redeemed Israel from Egypt for the express purpose of dwelling among them. God created Israel, just as God created the cosmos, in order to dwell within her.

The covenantal promise—"I will be your God and you will be my people, and I will dwell among you"—finds fulfillment in the church, which is the temple of God through the indwelling of the Spirit (1 Cor. 3:16; 2 Cor. 6:16). This indwelling anticipates the dwelling of God among redeemed humanity in the new heaven and new earth (Rev. 21:1-3). Through the indwelling Spirit we enjoy the communing presence of God whose Spirit transforms us. Our bodies are a divine sanctuary on earth, and the church is the sanctuary of God upon the earth. In this sense, we already experience what has not yet arrived.

Without diminishing the previous point, there is yet another dimension to this future-but-already-arrived presence of God. Hebrews 10:19-25 assures us that we enter the "Holy of Holies" of the heavenly tabernacle when we assemble to draw near to God. The Spirit who has descended into our hearts is the means by which we ascend into the heavenly tabernacle. There, we participate in the eschatological assembly around the throne of God (Heb. 12:18-24). Just as Israel met God at the earthly tabernacle in their great assemblies, so the church meets God in the heavenly tabernacle through their worshipping assemblies. The assembly of the church, then, participates in the future reality of the heavenly sanctuary. The assembly becomes a sanctuary of God on earth.

Conclusion

The story of the exodus is a sacramental journey. Israel experienced the gracious redemption of God as they passed through the waters, ate in the presence of God at the table, and worshipped at God's dwelling place in the tabernacle. As Israel passed through the sea, they were "baptized" into a new community. As they encamped around Sinai to "eat and drink" in the presence of God, they experienced the hospitality of God at the table. As they completed the tabernacle in which God came to dwell, they assembled "before the LORD" in a new way. Each of these moments lived in Israel's memory. They remembered their new baptismal identity in their worship, they communed with God through their fellowship meals, and they encountered God at the divine dwelling-place. In these moments they remembered and embodied their story with God.

The church, as the descendent of Israel, relives Israel's own sacramental moments through the church's sacraments. The church, grafted into Israel, celebrates the redemptive meaning of the exodus in our own baptism, continues to eat a thanksgiving meal at a table in God's presence, and comes "before the LORD" in the assembling of the saints. The story of salvation is one. God has acted and continues to act through the gracious gift of the sacraments. As Christians, we remember our baptismal identity, eat with God at the table, and encounter God when we assemble. Israel's sacramental journey is our own.

Chapter 2

THE MINISTRY OF JESUS:
From the Jordan to the Upper Room

Israel, blessed with the *shekinah* glory of God, settled in the promised land. Called to represent God among the nations and become their light, Israel was the renewed image of God in the world, a second Adam. Israel was to become what God intended for humanity, a testimony to God's intent for the whole creation. Consequently, Israel did not exist for its own sake but as a servant to the nations, to bless all nations.

Yet Israel hardened its heart. Instead of participating in God's mission, Israel followed the example of Genesis 3-11. They tumbled into the abyss of violence, injustice, and idolatry. Israel repeated the cycle of creation, fall, and exile in its own history. Just as Adam and Eve were exiled from Eden, so Israel was exiled from their land. Though some returned, with the exception of a brief period, Israel lived under oppressive empires for over five hundred years.

Israel was still living in exile when John the Baptizer appeared. Though the temple had been rebuilt, the glory of the Lord had not returned. The Davidic reign had not been restored. At the beginning of the first century they lived under the yoke of Roman oppression and prayed for the coming of the Messiah.

A New Exodus Through the Water

Jesus passed through the waters of Jordan, like Israel, to enter the wilderness. The Holy Spirit, whom God had poured out on Jesus at his baptism, led him into the wilderness. The crossing of the sea, the descent of God's presence, and forty years (days) of testing are re-presented in the life of Jesus.

The Baptismal Ministry of John (Luke 3)

John comes to Israel as the prophet of a new exodus. Isaiah 40 defined his mission. He is a prophetic voice "crying out in the wilderness" who plows the ground for the coming Messiah. Luke's citation of Isaiah includes 40:5, that is, "and all flesh shall see the salvation of God." Luke echoes this language in Acts 2:17-21 when he quotes the words of Joel's restoration: when God pours out the Spirit on "all flesh," "everyone who calls on the name of the Lord shall be saved." Pentecost was the restoration of Israel with the promise that "all flesh" would come to know God's salvation. It is an exodus for "all flesh."

John announces the coming kingdom of God as the fulfillment of God's promise to restore Israel. His mission and message are filled with the motifs and hopes of Jewish expectation.

Since Isaiah 40 announces Israel's exodus from Babylonian captivity, John is identifying his own ministry as preparation for a new exodus. The "last days" have arrived when God would liberate Israel from its oppression. God will end their exile. This is eschatological language. Something is about to change; God is doing a new work—a work of judgment and blessing. Little wonder then that John asked the "vipers" who had warned them "to flee from the wrath to come." God is about to come and "cut down" every tree that does not bear "good fruit" and throw it "into the fire."

John, therefore, calls for repentance. Those who would inherit the kingdom of God must repent. Those who come to him for baptism should share their possessions, pursue economic justice, and treat people fairly. Baptismal candidates must exhibit "fruits worthy of repentance." This resonates with the Jewish expectation of the "last days" and God's coming to restore penitent Israel. Joel called Israel to repentance. "Fire" devours the impenitent and the Spirit renews a remnant (Joel 1:19; 2:28-29). John has appeared at the end of days, the last of a long line of prophets, to call Israel to repentance.

John also has "good news" for Israel. His prophetic ministry creates a Messianic "expectation." The new exodus needs a new Moses. They wonder whether John himself is the Messiah. He is not, but the Messiah is coming and "he will baptize you with the Holy Spirit and fire." He will gather his people as he gathers wheat into a barn, but he will also winnow out the chaff and "burn it with unquenchable fire." The Messiah will execute judgment through a baptism in fire, but he will also bless his people through a baptism in the Spirit.

Herein lies the significance of baptism for John: a "baptism of repentance for the forgiveness of sins." John, as a baptizing prophet, initiates Israel into a new era, into the "last days." His baptism is a prophetic act—an act that both anticipates the coming Messianic age and effects the forgiveness of sins through faith-repentance. This repentance-baptism cleanses Israel in preparation for the Messiah's restoration of Israel. John administers this grace as God's prophet to proclaim God's saving work for Israel.

John's baptism is itself a new crossing. Against the backdrop of the wilderness, John baptizes in the Jordan that echoes the story of when God held back the waters of the Jordan so that Israel might enter the land. His baptism prepares Israel for the coming kingdom of God. It carries the symbolism of the exodus itself. Through John's baptism Israel crosses the Jordan once again but this time into a new era rather than a new land. They are entering the Messianic age.

John Baptizes Jesus

Luke's description of the baptism of Jesus is succinct, but filled with significant language (Luke 3:21-22).

> Now when all the people were baptized, and when Jesus also had been baptized and was praying, the heaven was opened, and the Holy Spirit descended upon him in bodily form like a dove. And a voice came from heaven, "You are my Son, the Beloved; with you I am well pleased."

Given the meaning of John's baptism, we are astonished to read that Jesus was baptized along with "all the people." The people and Jesus shared the same baptism—"a baptism of repentance for the forgiveness of sins." Jesus underwent a cleansing ritual. But why does Jesus need cleansing?

On the one hand, Jesus identified with Israel by undergoing a ritual designed for penitent sinners. Jesus joined those who were looking for the kingdom of God. This is, of course, exactly what Jesus did in his death. Quoting Isaiah 53:12, Jesus characterized himself as one "counted among the lawless" (Luke 22:37). When Jesus went down in the river, he counted himself among the lawless—not because he was himself a sinner, but because he identified with his people. He joined the penitent community that awaited the coming kingdom of God. He submitted to God's command as God's obedient servant.

On the other hand, Jesus experienced something that Israel had not yet known and would not know until the day of Pentecost. When Jesus was baptized, "the Holy Spirit descended upon him." In this moment, as Peter later recalled, Jesus was "anointed...with the Holy Spirit and with power" (Acts 10:38). This anointing involves several ideas. First, it promised divine presence. The Holy Spirit now abides with Jesus and leads him (Luke 4:1). Second, God commissioned Jesus. The Son is given the Messianic task—the Spirit-anointed task of the Messiah is to "preach good news to the poor" (Luke 4:18), and this anointing empowered Jesus for that task. Third, the anointing is a public declaration of God's relationship to Jesus. Jesus is God's beloved child.

Anointed by the Spirit at baptism Jesus committed himself to the way of the cross. Immediately after baptism, the Spirit led Jesus into the wilderness where he was tempted for forty days to turn from the way of the cross (Luke 4:1-13). But passing through the waters committed Jesus to his own baptism of suffering (Luke 12:50).

Jesus is a new Moses. He passed through the waters as a symbol of the new exodus. Like Israel, God affirmed him, loved him, and expressed pure delight in him at the waters. Like Israel, he was led into the wilderness by God's presence, the Spirit. Jesus was the suffering servant of God, a new Moses, who would lead Israel out of exile into abundance. Jesus passed through the waters, just like Israel passed through the sea, and then spent forty days in the wilderness just like Israel spent forty years there. Jesus' baptism inaugurated a new exodus.

Jesus' Baptism, Our Baptism

The baptism of Jesus has long been a central aspect of Christian imagination, piety, and art. The earliest piece of Christian art, and the most frequent scene depicted in the earliest centuries, is the baptism of Jesus. The Christian festival of Epiphany, celebrating the baptism of Jesus, was practiced in the East as early as the late second century, well before Christmas was ever instituted. By the late fourth century, Epiphany was the most significant feast in Syria. This emphasis was rooted in the belief that the baptism of Jesus was the "dominant model for Christian baptism."[1]

This is the first Christian baptism. Jesus is immersed in water, the Spirit is poured out on him, and God affirms Jesus as a beloved child. That is our baptism, too! Unfortunately, the baptism of Jesus is often relegated to the status of a mere example for believers at best and, at worst, an unrepeatable moment. But this public obedience on the part of Jesus is a pattern for us.

At one level, Jesus owned the divine mission in this act of surrender. Immersed by John, he surrendered his life to the purposes of God. Luke correlates the baptism and ministry of Jesus—Jesus is baptized and then he begins his ministry. At his baptism, Jesus becomes—in a significant sense—a disciple of God as he embraced the mission and ministry of the kingdom. He became a God-follower with a public ministry in the kingdom of God.

This is our baptism, too. When we are baptized, we own the divine mission as well. We surrender our will to the divine agenda, to the kingdom of God. We embody the prayer, "Your kingdom come; your will be done." We follow Jesus into the water to become Christ-followers, disciples of Jesus himself. Baptism is a discipleship marker—both in the life of Jesus and in our lives. If we follow Jesus into the water, then we must also follow him to the cross (Luke 9:23-26).

At another level, Jesus encountered God in this baptismal moment. Anointed by the Spirit, he heard the voice of God. What he heard is important—he is a beloved child in whom God delights. This is a profound declaration of deep joy and love rooted in Psalm 2:7, Isaiah 42:1, and Isaiah 62:4. It is a celebratory word from God as God rejoices over Jesus. Moreover, it is the inauguration of a renewed community—restored Israel. Jesus is the first member, the first fruit, of that community.

This is our baptism, too. When we are baptized, we encounter God. The words Jesus heard are not simply for him. They are about us as well. Arising out of the water we have become part of the community that God names "Hepzibah"—the one in whom God delights (Isa. 62:4). That is our name. We, too, are beloved children of God. The divine blessing voiced at the Jordan River is heard at every baptism. Like Jesus, we, too, are anointed with the Spirit. God's presence comes to dwell within us, transform us, and empower us. Like Jesus, we, too, become part of new Israel, a new community that welcomes the coming kingdom.

When I remember my baptism, I remember the baptism of Jesus. I remember that I committed myself to the way of the cross, the mission of God, and to the ministry of the kingdom. I remember that God poured out the Spirit upon me. I remember that God sang over me in that moment. God announced that I was a beloved child. Even now I hear the voice of God say— despite all my failures and faults—"You are my child," "You are loved," and "I am delighted with you!" God, even with my sins, celebrated me then and continues to rejoice over me now.

Jesus invites us to follow him, and if we would be disciples of Jesus, we will follow him into the water and know God's gracious delight and gifts. As we commit ourselves to the path of discipleship, God also acts in this moment—God delights, God declares, God anoints, and God forgives.

Baptism is about what God does. Through John, God announced the coming restoration of Israel and prepared a penitent and cleansed people. The Spirit-anointing of Jesus testifies to the reality of the "new age," a new exodus. The baptism of Jesus is, in some sense, the beginning of that "new age." God has acted to save Israel and the waters of Jesus' own baptism churn with eschatological fervor.

That is our baptism, too! When we are baptized, we, too, are anointed. When we are baptized, God says over us, "This is my child." When we are baptized, God rejoices over us.

Eating with Jesus in the Kingdom of God

Having passed through the waters and spent forty days in the wilderness, Jesus emerged from the Judean desert feasting rather than fasting. Jesus heralded the good news of the kingdom of God. The kingdom is near! The bridegroom has arrived. The disciples of Jesus, during his ministry, do not fast because they are no longer waiting for the Messiah. Instead, Jesus leads his disciples to tables where the present reality of the kingdom of God is experienced through feasting. The disciples of John and the Pharisees, still waiting for the kingdom, fast, but the disciples of Jesus—while the bridegroom is with them—rejoice at the table. The table of Jesus is a witness to the presence of the kingdom of God (Mark 2:13-22).

The Table Ministry of Jesus (Luke 9)

The table ministry of Jesus is often ignored in framing our understanding of the Lord's supper. For some it seems too removed from the Last Supper and for others the Lord's supper is a highly formalized ritual unlike the tables in Jesus' ministry. However, in the Gospel of Luke the Last Supper is linked with the other tables by language and content.

Luke is a narrator. He tells stories, and each meal story reveals something about Jesus and his mission. In Luke 5:27-32, Jesus sits at table with sinners as a physican among the sick. In Luke 7:36-50, Jesus receives a sinful woman at the table of a Pharisee and forgives her sins. In Luke 10:38-42, Jesus accepts women as disciples. In Luke 11:37-54, Jesus condemns the Pharisees because they sit at table only in form, not in spirit. In Luke 14:1-24, the table of Jesus' host does not look like the kingdom of God; it looks like them. In Luke 19:1-10, Jesus eats with the tax collector Zacchaeus to announce that salvation had come to his house.

At table, Jesus receives sinners and confronts the righteous. At table, Jesus extends grace to seekers but condemns the self-righteous. Jesus eats with "others" to introduce them to the kingdom. He contrasts our tables of social, ethnic, gender, economic, and religious status with the table in the kingdom of God. The last (sinners, poor, and humbled—the "others") will be first in the kingdom of God, but the first (self-righteous, rich, and proud—the religious elite) will be last in the kingdom of God (Luke 13:26-30). The table is missional, communal, and hospitable.

The feeding of the five thousand in Luke 9:10-17 is particularly significant for several reasons. First, it is the only meal in Luke prior to the Last Supper where Jesus is the host. Second, it contains language that is explicitly tied to the Last Supper. Third, the Messiah, as a new Moses, feeds his people in the wilderness.

Jesus sent "the twelve" out to "preach the kingdom of God and to heal" the sick (Luke 9:1-2). Upon their return, Jesus retires with them to Bethsaida. Between their sending and return, Luke injects a question in the mouth of Herod the tetrarch that shapes the following narrative: "Who is this about whom I hear such things" (Luke 9:9). This question, "Who is Jesus?" asked both before and after the feeding in the wilderness dominates this section of Scripture. Peter confidently answers the question in Luke 9:20, "The Messiah of God." He, like all the people, interprets the hospitality, preaching, healing, and feeding of the people as significant Messianic signs.

The meal story, then, identifies Jesus as the Messiah who hosts a meal with his disciples. In this banquet, the Messiah welcomes the crowd and proclaims the kingdom of God. Jesus, as Messiah, feeds the people of God in the wilderness ("deserted place"), just as Moses fed Israel with manna in the wilderness. The table confirms Jesus as God's anointed one. The meal is characterized by joy, abundance, and compassion as Jesus feeds the hungry. It is a meal in the wilderness for a people seeking the kingdom of God, their inheritance.

This meal anticipates the Passover meal in Luke 22. There is a direct link between the two as the same themes and language are present in both texts. Particularly compelling is the fact that the same liturgical language—Jesus *took* the bread, *blessed* it, *broke* it and *gave* it—is used in both meals. Both this feeding and the Last Supper are kingdom meals that anticipate the fullness of the Messianic banquet in the new heaven and new earth. Like manna in the wilderness, Jesus breaks the "bread of heaven" in both Luke 9 and Luke 22.

Topic	Luke 9	Luke 22
Kingdom Language	Spoke about the kingdom	Fulfillment in the Kingdom
Twelve	Twelve Apostles/Baskets	Twelve Tribes/Apostles
Israel/Exodus/Wilderness	Manna in the Wilderness	Exodus Memorial Meal
Disciples Disputing	Who's the Greatest?	Who's the Greatest?
Reclining (at table)	Table Etiquette	Table Etiquette
Liturgical Formula	Took, Blessed, Broke, Gave	Took, Blessed, Broke, Gave
Jesus as Host	Host in the Wilderness	Host at the Passover
Hospitality (Lodging)	Providing Hospitality	Accepting Hospitality
Apostolic Mission	Traveling Missionaries	Judging the Tribes
Eating a Meal	Loaves and Fishes	Passover Lamb
Service	Disciples Serve	Jesus Serves

The meal stories have theological meaning for Luke's community, and they shaped meals in the early church. The table ministry of Jesus continued in the church. It revealed a new kingdom etiquette. Since the Lord's supper is the Lord's kingdom table, the table etiquette of the ministry of Jesus also informs the table in the church.

Last Supper (Luke 22)

Most people associate the Lord's supper with the Last Supper. Described by three Gospels (Mark 14; Matthew 26; Luke 22) and remembered by Paul (1 Corinthians 11:17-34), the Last Supper is where Jesus imagined future meals with his disciples. "Do this in remembrance of me," he commanded.

Luke's Last Supper is a Passover meal. Not only does this underscore the continuity between Israel's fellowship meals and what Jesus institutes, it also creates an air of expectancy and hope. Passover meals looked forward to the coming of the kingdom of God. Jesus himself makes the link. The Passover meal will not only find its fulfillment in the kingdom of God, but Jesus will enjoy it with his disciples when the kingdom of God comes. The new covenant meal extends the meaning of Passover: now the exodus of Israel from Egypt is celebrated alongside a new exodus. Though the Last Supper points back to Israel's liberation, it also embraces a future liberation from sin, death, and cosmic bondage. The Last Supper, as the inauguration of a new meal (the fulfilled Passover), is a meal that participates in the future Messianic banquet of the new heaven and new earth.

Luke's language, however, is best understood through the lens of an already/not yet eschatology. Jesus will eat with his disciples when the kingdom comes but it will come both within history and when history reaches its goal. In other words, Jesus will eat with his disciples in the new community that will emerge on the day of Pentecost and eat with his disciples at the eschatological Messianic banquet (Isa. 25:6-9).

The traditional essence of the Lord's supper is the bread and wine liturgy. The actions and words of Jesus are important: He (1) *took bread*, (2) *gave thanks*, (3) *broke* it, and (4) *gave* it to the disciples (and a similar action with the cup). This deliberate construction (repeated elsewhere in Luke) is significant. The four-fold structure highlights a Passover ritual which carries the meaning of eating and drinking itself. We gratefully receive and share God's gifts of bread and wine.

What does Jesus mean when he says, "This is my body" and "This is my blood"? The language certainly interprets the meal. They give new meaning to the Passover without sub-verting its previous meaning. Just as the bread of the Passover represented life and liberation, so the body of Jesus gives life and liberation. Bread is what nourishes life, and the body of Christ nourishes believers. Bread is life, and it is shared life. The community's life is grounded in the gift of Christ's body. In effect, Jesus says "my body" will give new life to Israel. "My body" is the basis and reality of a new exodus.

The cup is, Jesus says, "the new covenant in my blood" which is "poured out for you." The blood of the Passover lamb gives new life. Jesus' blood is covenantal blood; it enacts covenant. Jesus alludes to the moment when God entered into covenant with Israel at Mt. Sinai (Exod. 24:8), and we should hear the echoes of eating with God on Sinai (Exod. 24:11). Jesus is the slaughtered lamb who pours out his life and bears the sin of many (Isa. 53:12). "My blood" is the basis and reality of the new exodus.

Jesus gives the Passover meal a new horizon of meaning. The Passover lamb died to liberate the firstborn from death and bring Israel out of Egyptian bondage. Jesus, as the true Lamb of God, gives new life and frees us from sin and death through his death. The original meaning of the Passover remains, but it is transformed by the new reality that is grounded in the death of Jesus.

At the same time, Jesus expects to eat and drink again with his disciples in the kingdom of God. Death is not the final word. Though he offers his body and blood through death, Jesus hosts the table as the living Christ. Though he dies, he yet lives again to share this table with his disciples in the kingdom of God. The table, then, is not simply about the death of Jesus. Through his resurrected life, Jesus will host the kingdom table.

When we eat and drink at the table of the Lord, we experience both life and forgiveness. It is a table of mercy and grace. But it is also a table of commitment. As we drink the cup, we commit ourselves to the way of the cross. As we eat the bread, we share a communal life that is shaped by the ministry of Jesus. When we eat and drink together, we recommit ourselves to that way of life. When we eat and drink we renew covenant with God in Jesus and, in effect, do what Israel did in Exodus 24. We say, "Yes, we will live by the covenant!"

The table, therefore, calls us into the ministry of Jesus. At the Last Supper Jesus was not simply *at* the table, but he *served* the table. Jesus was the deacon (*diakonon*) of the Last Supper table. Jesus was not only the host, but also the waiter. This was no freak occurrence as if it were a blip on the screen. Just as Jesus served his disciples at the table, so the returning Son will serve his servants at the table when God spreads the Messianic banquet for humanity. "Blessed are those slaves whom the master finds alert when he comes," Jesus says, "truly I tell you, he will fasten his belt and have them sit down to eat, and he will come and serve (*diakonesei*) them" (Luke 12:37).

The table is not about power, control, or authority. Neither clerical authority nor gender prerogatives have a place at the table. It is about mutual service and ministry. The table is where we serve each other, and it is where we commit ourselves to the servant ministry of Jesus. Just as Jesus served us at the altar (cross) and continues to serve us at the table (nourishing and forgiving us), so we serve each other and the world.

We eat and drink, however, not in morbid reflection on the horrors of the cross but as participants in the new life that is the kingdom of God. The kingdom of God in Luke is not only about the Messianic banquet in the new heaven and new earth, but it is also about the in-breaking of the kingdom of God in the present. The living Christ is the reality of the kingdom of God, and thus the bread and wine are the reality of that kingdom now. In this new existence, Jesus eats and drinks with us. We eat and drink with the living Christ whose body nourishes us so that we might serve others and whose blood transforms death into life so that we might have hope.

Post-Resurrection Table (Luke 24)

Early Easter morning, Friday loomed large in the hearts of the disciples. Israel was still in exile. There was no exodus. Injustice and violence had won once again. Or, so it appeared.

During the Last Supper Jesus promised that he would eat and drink with his disciples again when the kingdom of God had come. Three days later, on the first day of the week, Jesus eats with his disciples. The kingdom of God, in some sense, arrived in the resurrection of Jesus. The presence of the resurrected Jesus is the presence of the future kingdom. To eat and drink with Jesus, then, is to experience the kingdom. The table transforms death into life and despair into hope. It is the joy of a new exodus, an exodus from death into life.

This is what the disciples experienced on that first Sunday after the crucifixion. The previous Friday had destroyed their hope. Calvary was a defeat. The one they had hoped was Israel's Messiah was dead. They still believed he was a good man, a miracle-worker, even a prophet. But they had lost hope that he was the Messiah. A dejected and hopeless pair of disciples walked from Jerusalem to Emmaus on that first day of the week.

As they walked, Jesus joined them, though "their eyes were kept from recognizing him." It was not yet time to see him. Instead, they told Jesus everything that had happened over the past few days. They confessed their hopelessness and skepticism. Jesus invited them to believe the prophets, and he explained the Scriptures. Jesus interpreted the events of the last three days—the cross and the resurrection are the suffering and glory of the Messiah.

As they neared Emmaus, the two disciples urged Jesus to lodge with them. Though the disciples were the hosts, their guest assumed the honors. This is only the third meal in Luke where Jesus served as host. The other two are the feeding of the five thousand (Luke 9) and the Last Supper (Luke 22).

Jesus' actions at this table exactly parallel the other two meals he hosted. Jesus "*took* bread, *blessed* and *broke* it, and *gave* it to them." Luke's language unites the meals. Jesus once again eats with his disciples in the first post-resurrection Eucharist. The narrative clues are abundant: he said he would eat with them and he did, Luke uses the same language to describe the breaking of the bread, Jesus is the host, and the meaning of the meal is the life of Jesus. As a narrator, Luke identifies this meal with the Last Supper. On Easter evening, the disciples of Jesus experienced their first "Lord's supper" with the resurrected Christ.

Most significantly, in the breaking of the bread, Jesus was "made known" to the disciples. They now "recognized" him; "their eyes were opened." They encountered the living Christ. Like Israel on Mt. Sinai in Exodus 24, they "saw" God. Friday disappeared and Sunday emerged as a joyous celebration. The significance of this moment was not lost on the two disciples. They had seen the risen Lord, and they quickly returned to Jerusalem to tell the other disciples. Then Jesus appeared to the whole group, and he ate with them and studied Scripture with them.

The table is a table of hope as it declares the presence of the kingdom through the resurrection of Jesus. The living host is present at the table eating and drinking with his disciples. The table on that first Sunday was a table of joy and celebration. There were no hearts burdened with sadness at that Easter table.

Luke 24, as a narrative model of the Lord's supper, informs the practice of the church. The Word and table are the focal points of the story, and they are the focus of Christian worship assemblies. The Word interprets the table as the table embodies the Word. The table without the Word is subject to misunderstanding, and the Word without the table misses the experience of the living Christ as host. The two belong together.

The church affirms and enjoys the resurrection of Jesus at the table. At the table we recognize the victory of the resurrection as we eat and drink in hope with the living Christ. At the table we leave all our "Fridays" behind us and celebrate the victory of Christ on Sunday. The table transforms "Friday" into "Sunday." Unfortunately, the church still generally practices the supper as if it were still Friday rather than Sunday. But through the supper we celebrate Sunday and God's victory over Friday. Sunday reinterprets and renews our Fridays. Why, then, does the church eat on Sunday as if it is still Friday?

Conclusion

Jesus passed through the waters and into the wilderness. Coming out of the wilderness he announced Jubilee and heralded the good news of the kingdom of God in both word and deed. Jesus embodied the kingdom of God by sitting at table with "others" as well as the privileged. He hosted a table for five thousand that imitated Moses feeding Israel in the wilderness. He reinterpreted the Passover as a new exodus through his body and blood. He broke bread with his disciples on the first day of the week to reveal that he had passed through death to new life. God released Jesus from the bondage of death, and a new creation, a new exodus, began. This is what Jesus reveals and shares with his disciples when he breaks bread with them.

As disciples of Jesus, we follow Jesus into the water and embrace his mission as our own. We follow Jesus into the wilderness where our loyalty is tested and our hearts are strengthened. We follow Jesus to the tables of ministry where we welcome "others" and call the "righteous" to repentance. As disciples of Jesus, we break bread with Jesus in the kingdom of God. The living host assures us that though we face suffering and death for the sake of the kingdom we will yet live with him. Just as the Messiah himself, we too must first suffer and then enter into glory. The story of Jesus is our story.

Chapter 3

ACTS: From Jerusalem to the Ends of the Earth

The Gospel of Luke ends and the Book of Acts begins with the ascension of Jesus to the right hand of God. This movement is not so much about spatial relocation as it is enthronement. The resurrected Messiah ascended to the throne. Daniel 7 describes the Son of Man coming with the clouds and assuming the throne of the everlasting kingdom. The Messiah is given "dominion and glory and kingship, that all peoples, nations, and languages should serve him" (Dan. 7:14). Jesus' obedient service at the cross was vindicated by his resurrection from the dead that he might assume the reins of the kingdom of God.

Luke also ends and Acts begins with a small community of disciples waiting in Jerusalem. Already immersed in the water of John's baptism, they anticipate their baptism in Spirit.

This baptism will immerse them in the presence of God and empower them as witnesses not only in Jerusalem and Judea, but also in Samaria, and to the ends of the earth (Acts 1:8). Just as Jesus was anointed with the Spirit as he came out of the water, these disciples wait for their own anointing. Their anointing is no individualistic reception of the Spirit, but an immersion into a new community upon which the Spirit has been poured.

God chose Pentecost for that outpouring. Following fifty days after the Passover, Pentecost was the "eighth day" of the seventh week. It was, in effect, the day of new creation, the first day of a new week. The festival celebrated the spring harvest, and the first fruits were offered to God. In Acts 2, the Spirit of God is poured out upon a waiting community as the first fruits of a renewed Israel, as the first fruits of a new creation. The Spirit, as in Genesis 1, hovers over the chaos of the human condition to create anew.

The enthroned Messiah receives from the Father the promised Holy Spirit who is poured out on restored Israel. His enthronement at the right of hand of God, raised to sit on the throne of David, gives birth to the descent of the Spirit. This descent is the indwelling of God within new Israel. Just as God dwelt in the tabernacle in the midst of Israel, so now God dwells in the church through the Spirit. The people of God are now the temple of the Lord. Pentecost is the fulfillment of the fuller promise embedded in God's descent upon the tabernacle in Exodus 40. Pentecost, from one perspective, is the goal of the new exodus, that is, that God might dwell in the midst of renewed Israel, the new creation.

How does one participate in renewed Israel? The brief answer is trust in Jesus, pass through the waters with Jesus, and share the communal journey through the wilderness into new heaven and new earth. The gift of the Spirit marks one as a member of this renewed people. Acts 2 provides a succinct description. Three thousand were "added" to the community through baptism, and "they devoted themselves" to life in community, including the "breaking of bread."

Baptized in the Name of Jesus (Acts 2)

Faced with the horror that they had killed the Messiah and recognizing the fulfillment of Joel 2, some were "cut to the heart" and wanted to know what to do. Peter's response probably sounded rather familiar but yet new: "Repent, and be baptized every one of you in the name of Jesus Christ so that your sins may be forgiven; and you will receive the gift of the Holy Spirit" (Acts 2:38). Penitent Israel once again must pass through the waters that God might dwell among them.

What Shall We Do?

Acts 2 is easily skewed. *On the one hand,* some focus on the chapter's baptismal language and leave the impression that the main point is baptism. *On the other hand,* others fail to see how significant Acts 2:38-39 is for the announcement of the restoration of Israel. The former tend to lift Acts 2:38 out of its context so that it has a quasi-independent function while the latter do not connect it with the language of restoration found in the narrative.

Peter's sermon announced the beginning of the "last days." What the prophet Joel foretold and what John the Baptist predicted, Peter declared a reality. God has poured out the Spirit to renew Israel. Salvation has come to Israel—to "everyone who calls on the name of the Lord"—and this salvation is evidenced by the presence of the Spirit. These events were fulfilling everything that Jesus had announced earlier: repentance and forgiveness were being preached in the name of the Lord to all nations in the power of the Spirit (Luke 24:46-49).

The response to Peter's pressing question, "What shall we do?" in Acts 2:38 summarizes the human response to the gospel in Luke's narrative. Joel Green counsels us to take "with the greatest seriousness the pattern-setting words of Peter in Acts 2:38."[1] Just as the baptism of Jesus functions as a model in Luke's narrative, these words have a normative import in Acts. Peter's call for repentance and baptism is analogous to John's call for repentance and baptism. Both seek to prepare a people for God's presence and the arrival of the kingdom of God. But it is different for Peter. He promises not only the forgiveness of sins, but also the presence of the Holy Spirit. Whereas John's baptism was a baptism of repentance for the forgiveness of sins, Peter announces a baptism of repentance for the forgiveness of sins with the subsequent reception of the Holy Spirit.

The normative human response to the announcement that God invites us into this renewed community is faith, repentance, and baptism. God has restored Israel and poured out the Spirit upon it. If we take this normative perspective seriously as a narrative indicator, then "even when Luke does not

enumerate each item of human response and salvific promise comprised in Peter's pronouncement (and he rarely does),
those responses and salvific gifts are to be presumed present
unless we are given explicit reason to think otherwise."[2]

Though specific grammatical points have been hotly con-
tested (e.g., the meaning of *eis* or whether "for the remission
of sins" modifies the verb "baptized"), the most significant
function of Acts 2:38-39 is sometimes neglected. Joel proph-
esied that God would pour out the Spirit on "all flesh" (Acts
2:17), and John's work prepared the way for "all flesh" to see
God's salvation (Luke 3:6). Peter announces that those who
repent and are baptized in the name of Jesus will receive the
promise of the Holy Spirit, the epitome of a redeemed people.
To be baptized "in (*epi*) the name" of Jesus is to participate in
restored Israel as people who "call on (*epikalesetai*) the name
of the Lord" (Acts 2:21, 38). They are baptized "upon the name
of Jesus" as they "call upon" the name of Jesus for salvation
(Acts 22:16). These baptized believers from all over the world
constitute a new community as restored Israel. As others are
baptized in the "name of Jesus," the Samaritans in Acts 8:16
or the Gentiles ('the ends of the earth") in Acts 10:48, they,
too, join that same community. The restored people of God
transcend ethnic and social boundaries; it includes "all flesh."

The "promise" belongs to this community (Acts 2:39),
including the "promise" of the Holy Spirit (cf. Acts 2:33) and
much more. The promised Spirit is evidence of the fulfillment
of God's promises to Abraham, including the promise that
his seed would bless all nations. The presence of the Spirit is
a partial fulfillment, a down payment of sorts, which looks

forward to the full implementation of God's promises when the people of God inherit the cosmos (Rom 4:13). This new community, the church, is the heir of Abraham through the work of the Messiah.

The Conversion of Saul

Besides Cornelius (Acts 10, 11, 15), no other conversion narrative receives as much attention as the conversion of Saul (Acts 9, 22, 26), which legitimates Paul's standing as an apostle to the Gentiles whom God has included in restored Israel (Acts 9:15-16; 22:21; 26:17-18). Consequently, the primary focus is not to provide a "pattern" for the sequence of conversion events but to bear witness to God's intent that restored Israel would include "all flesh" (Acts 2:17) and that witnesses should go to the "ends of the earth" (Acts 1:8).

At the same time, Saul's story illustrates the connected nature of faith, repentance, baptism, forgiveness of sins, and the Holy Spirit that is characteristic of Acts. As an enemy of Christianity, Saul intended to persecute believers in Damascus, but on his way there he encountered the risen Messiah. He was struck blind and led into Damascus by his companions. For three days he fasted as he devoted himself to penitent prayer (Acts 9:9, 11). Then the Lord sent Ananias.

Ananias explained to Saul that he had come that "you may regain your sight and be filled with the Holy Spirit" (Acts 9:17). When Ananias laid his hands on him, he received his sight. Then Ananias announced that Saul was God's chosen witness to "all the world" and asked him, "And now why do you delay? Get up, be baptized, and have your sins washed away, calling on his name" (Acts 22:15-16). Paul got up and was baptized (Acts 9:18).

When was Paul converted? Does "converted" mean when his sins were forgiven or when he became a believer? Are we even to think in terms of a specific moment in time? The narrative must be read as a whole rather than piecemeal. It tells the story of an unbeliever who becomes a believer and seeks the Lord through intense prayer for three days, and a servant of God then heals and baptizes this penitent believer. If "conversion" means the whole process of becoming a Christian, Saul's healing and baptism after three days of prayer and fasting was the climactic moment. If, however, we are asking when he became a believer in the risen Messiah, then it was on the road to Damascus. The narrative is about the transformation of an enemy of the cross into God's witness to the Gentile world. The process is significant, but it is a process filled with events—Saul "sees" Jesus on the road to Damascus, he fasts and prays for three days, he is healed, and he is baptized.

We should not undervalue any of these moments. On the one hand, those who emphasize baptism as the point at which Saul's sins were forgiven undervalue the transformative nature of his experience with the risen Messiah. Saul was a changed person before his baptism. He had come to faith in Jesus. On the other hand, some who emphasize his experience on the Damascus road as the converting moment undervalue the significance of his healing and baptism as the conclusion of the conversion narrative when Paul is assured of his relationship with Jesus and is received as a member of the Christian community.

When did Paul receive the Holy Spirit? He did not receive the Spirit on the Damascus road because Ananias came that Paul might receive the Spirit. But did Paul receive the Holy Spirit when he was healed as Ananias laid his hands on him? Or, did he receive the Holy Spirit when he was baptized? From the perspective of Acts 2:38, we might argue the latter, but the narrative offers no decisive answer to those questions. Rather, the narrative assumes that faith, repentance, baptism, forgiveness, and the reception of the Spirit are parts of the whole. Whatever the sequence, the conversion narrative involved all of the above and was incomplete without any of them.

This is consistent with other conversion narratives in Acts (8:11-13, 35-36; 16:14-15, 32-33; 18:8; 19:5). Baptism immediately follows believing the gospel. Baptism was the concrete way in which the gospel was received. Luke tells his story in such a way that the conversion narrative has constitutive elements. Even when these are not explicitly mentioned in every case, his narrative world assumes them. Luke, as a narrator, intends to provide a holistic picture— conversion is our initiation into the community of faith. The conversion narrative in Acts involves faith, repentance, and baptism as hearers respond to the gracious message of God's saving work in Christ.

This is rather different than the conversion narrative popular among many contemporary revivalists. Nowhere does one read in Scripture that conversion is asking Jesus into one's heart through the "sinner's prayer." Rather, the one who would call upon the name of Lord is baptized upon the name of Jesus. Ananias summons Paul to "arise and be baptized . . . calling upon the name of the Lord" (Acts 22:16). In Acts, baptism *is* the "sinner's prayer."

The Gift of the Holy Spirit

In Luke's narrative, people hear the message of the gospel, believe it, are immersed in response to it, and enjoy its benefits. Some of these elements are present in some stories, but not in others (e.g., explicit references to repentance). While Luke's purpose does not demand a consistent, repetitive retelling of conversion stories in some kind of standardized language, his consistency is fairly telling.

However, there is one element that is clearly problematic: there is no consistent pattern in the book of Acts regarding the reception of the Spirit. Those baptized on Pentecost received the Holy Spirit as a promise connected *with* baptism (Acts 2:38). Those baptized in Samaria received the Holy Spirit a significant time *after* baptism (Acts 8:15-17). Those baptized at Cornelius' house received the Holy Spirit *before* baptism (Acts 10:47).

Which of these accounts is the *ordinary* pattern of God's work? Perhaps it is inappropriate to find an "ordinary" pattern. After all, God is free to distribute the Spirit as God wills. Nothing constrains God's gift except God's own decision. Furthermore, it is inappropriate to impose on Luke's stories a grid that determines the "ordinary" order when he is unconcerned about that point. Thus, whether there is an "ordinary" pattern or order depends upon Luke's own narrative.

Though his narrative contains an inordinate pattern regarding baptism and the Holy Spirit, Luke seems to recognize that two of his stories are extraordinary because he explains them. His editorial comment in Acts 8:16 indicates that Luke is aware that this is an anomalous situation. That the Samaritans did not receive the Spirit when they were baptized needed explanation (Acts 8:15). Luke explains why Peter and John were present to give the Spirit because the reader, based on Acts 2:38, might have expected that they would have received the Spirit with their baptism. Luke recognizes the exceptional nature of the situation. He does not explain the difference in terms of a supposed distinction between the "miraculous" and "ordinary" gift of the Spirit. Rather, he specifically states that they did not receive the Holy Spirit. The exceptional circumstance appears directly related to their ethnic and social standing as Samaritans. God, through Peter and John, bore witness to the inclusion of the Samaritans within restored Israel (Acts 1:8).

Luke also appears to indicate that the circumstance of Cornelius is extraordinary. Cornelius was an uncircumcised Gentile, and no uncircumcised person had ever been included within Israel. God poured out the Spirit upon the house of Cornelius before he was either baptized or circumcised. As a result Peter asked, "Can anyone withhold the water for baptizing these people who have received the Holy Spirit just as we have?" (Acts 10:47). God's action bore witness to the fact that he accepted the inclusion of uncircumcised Gentiles within restored Israel. When his Jerusalem brothers objected, Peter asked, "If then God gave them the same gift that he gave us when we believed in the Lord Jesus Christ, who was I that I could hinder God?" (Acts 11:17). The significance of this extraordinary situation is highlighted by the fact that Luke defends the inclusion of uncircumcised Gentiles by rehearsing the story of Cornelius' conversion three times (Acts 10, 11 and 15). Since God poured his Spirit on Cornelius they could not be denied baptism and thus inclusion in the community since the presence of the Spirit is the mark of community membership.

Despite the fact that these situations are extraordinary and that Acts 2:38 probably functions as the ordinary means, we should not underestimate the significance of God's use of extraordinary situations or means. God is sovereign. God gives the Spirit when, where, and to whomever God desires. God is not bound to ordinary means. We may rest upon God's promise in Acts 2:38, but God is not limited by Acts 2:38 in the distribution of the Spirit.

Further, recognizing this diversity in Luke's narrative alerts us to something exceedingly more important. Luke's main concern was not baptism. Rather, Luke is much more concerned with the presence, work, and power of the Spirit. Baptism serves the larger theme of a restored community indwelt and empowered by the Spirit. Too often, based on Acts 2:38 and our search for the assurance of forgiveness, we orient Luke's narrative to baptism as if this was his primary point. But if we recognize that the "pouring out of the Spirit" upon restored Israel was Luke's primary point, then baptism, while important, assumes a secondary role.

When we think of the gift of the Spirit and baptism, we must recognize that the presence of the Spirit is more important than baptism. Just by a nose count, Luke gives more emphasis to the Spirit than to baptism by a three to one margin. But a word count is not the main indicator. Rather, it is the link between the pouring out of the Spirit and the restoration of Israel. The salvation of Israel is the presence of God's cleansing and empowering Spirit. The presence of the Spirit is the evidence of God's new creation.

Yet, despite this caveat, Luke's theology expects that baptism and the giving of the Spirit come in close proximity. When the baptized Samaritans do not have the Spirit, Luke explains the anomaly. When an unbaptized Cornelius receives the Spirit, Luke explains the circumstance. In both episodes, baptism and the Spirit were expected correlates, and, though separated, the narrative ultimately united them—everyone who received the Spirit was baptized and everyone who was baptized received the Spirit. Conversion, baptism, and the Holy Spirit are interwoven. Luke's narrative connects them, and no conversion narrative leaves the impression that there might be a Christian who has the Spirit but is unbaptized or that there is one who is baptized but has not received the Spirit. When either is the case, the other follows in order to complete the conversion.

Breaking Bread with Jesus

Having passed through the waters and received the gift of God's presence, renewed Israel now looks toward its inheritance, the promised land. The journey through the wilderness is treacherous and dangerous, but a community devoted to God's guidance and facing the dangers together will reach the promised land. This is the story of the church in Acts.

The Jerusalem Church

Three thousand people were immersed on Pentecost Sunday, and they formed a new community. These Jesus-followers "devoted themselves to the apostles' teaching and fellowship, to the breaking of bread and to prayers" (Acts 2:42). The structure of Acts 2:42 is ambiguous. Luke may describe four different activities: (1) teaching, (2) fellowship, (3) breaking of bread, and (4) prayers. Or, and more probably, he is describing two main activities, (1) teaching and (2) fellowship, and then fellowship is subdivided as (a) breaking bread and (b) prayers. The text does not list four successive elements, each linked with "and" (*kai*). Rather, the first two are linked as correlate activities and the last two are linked by "and," but the two sets are not so linked. Luke, I think, intends us to read "breaking of bread" and "prayers" as two forms of fellowship.

If this is correct, Luke subsumes the "breaking of bread" under fellowship (*koinonia*). Breaking bread is communion, a communally shared meal. But this is not all that the disciples shared. They also shared their possessions. They "had all things in common" (*koina*). The early disciples experienced *koinonia* through shared meals and shared wealth. The fellowship of the disciples was concrete and visible rather than just "spiritual" and invisible. The love of the disciples meant that they shared their lives including food and material possessions.

If we recognize that Pentecost is Israel's new exodus, then this new community begins a new journey in the shadow of Mt. Zion. Like Israel, they must wander through the wilderness of a frustrated creation in the hope of inheriting the whole world in the new creation. The Spirit of God, who dwells in their midst, leads this new community just as the pillar of cloud and fire led Israel in the wilderness. Like Israel, they share life and food on their journey, including the breaking of bread.

But what does "breaking bread" mean? Luke's Gospel provides the context for this phrase in Acts. Three times Luke describes Jesus' actions as host where he *takes* the bread, *blesses* it, *breaks* it, and *gives* it to his disciples. When he cryptically refers to the "breaking of bread" in Acts, he assumes the reader knows the fuller stories of his Gospel (in much the same way that there is no need to explain the Shire in Tolkien's second volume when it had been thoroughly described in the first). Luke assumes the readers of Acts understand the theological significance of "breaking bread" because of what he had written in the Gospel. That significance is defined by Luke 24:35 which is the "hinge" text for the "breaking of bread" stories.

The Gospel of Luke	Hinge Text	The Book of Acts
Luke 9:16 Jesus took bread, blessed, broke and gave it.		Acts 2:42 the disciples continued in the breaking of bread
Luke 22:19 Jesus took bread, gave thanks, broke and gave it.	Luke 24:35 Jesus was "made known to them in the breaking of the bread"	Acts 2:46 the disciples broke bread daily in their homes
Luke 24:30 Jesus took bread, blessed, broke and gave it.		Acts 20:7 the disciples gathered to break bread

The early church, as a community, celebrated the presence of Christ through breaking bread (cf. 1 Cor. 10:16). In the light of Luke's Gospel, the breaking of bread refers to a meal with

Jesus where his living presence is revealed. When the disciples "broke bread" they experienced Christ's presence at the table as host.

Acts 2:41-47 summarizes the life of this new Israel. It models Christian community and provides a reference point for the development of Christian life and practice throughout the whole of Acts. In particular, Acts 2:42 serves as a thesis statement for the rest of chapter two. The disciples "devoted themselves to the apostles' teaching" because of the "wonders and signs" they performed (Acts 2:43). The disciples also devoted themselves to "fellowship," and they shared their possessions with the needy (Acts 2:44-45). In summary fashion, Luke concretizes Acts 2:42 by describing the daily experience of the Jerusalem church in Acts 2:46-47.

> Day by day, as they spent much time together in the temple, they broke bread at home and ate their food with glad and generous hearts, praising God and having the good will of all the people. And day by day the Lord added to their number those who were being saved.

Restored Israel gathered daily in the temple and in homes. Presumably, given the activities in the rest of Acts, they gathered in the temple for prayers and the teaching of the apostles (cf. Acts 3:1; 5:21, 42).

They gathered daily in homes for fellowship through breaking bread. They shared food with joy and generosity. There is no reason to distinguish between the breaking of bread in Acts 2:42 and Acts 2:46—they refer to a meal in which the liturgical pattern was enacted [taking, breaking, blessing, and giving bread], the Lord was remembered, and his presence celebrated. The structural connectedness (for example, a series of verbs in the imperfect tense) of Acts 2:41-47 means that 2:42 and 2:46 refer to the same kind of "breaking bread." Whatever this "breaking bread" is ought to be interpreted against the background of Luke 9, 22, and 24 so that those texts inform our understanding of Acts 2. It is incredulous that Luke would use the same language ("breaking bread") to describe two different things within the space of five verses. Consequently, "breaking bread" in Acts 2:42 and 2:46 refer to the Lord's supper, a daily meal in the Jerusalem church.

Since "food" was eaten in this breaking of bread, the Lord's supper was a meal. Indeed, it was a concrete form of *koinonia*. The disciples not only shared their material possessions with those in need, they shared their food as well. The Lord's supper had a social function. In this way, the church shared food with the poor in their community and offered hospitality to others as they proclaimed the gospel through their meals together.

This economic dimension of sharing food with the needy explains the "daily" dimension of "breaking bread." It is part of what the community held in "common" (Acts 2:44; 4:32) so that there were no needy persons among them (Acts 4:34). In this way, the new Israel embodied the Torah regulations of Deuteronomy 15:1-11. "Breaking bread" was central to this daily experience as disciples gathered to commune with each other by sharing food in the presence of the living Christ. If the Lord's supper is understood as a meal, then its "daily" character is understandable; people must eat. The Lord's supper, then, was not a mere corporate worship ritual, but the daily experience of praising God in a community of disciples who ate together.

Breaking Bread in Troas

Narrating Paul's return to Jerusalem on his third missionary journey with a collection of money for the poor, Luke's travelogue includes a story about breaking bread in Troas (Acts 20:7-12). The intentional character of "breaking bread" is obvious. The community gathered in order "to break bread." This was its explicit purpose for assembling. Paul's sermon was an addendum or special circumstance.

Topic	Luke 24	Acts 20
Gathering of Disciples	24:33	20:7
Breaking of Bread	24:30,35	20:7,11
Eating Together	24:42-43	20:11
First Day of the Week	24:1,13	20:7
Teaching the Word (*logos*)	24:44	20:7
Conversation (*omileo*)	24:14-15	20:11
A Rising from the Dead	24:5,46	20:10,12
Fear	24:37-38	20:11
The Living One (*zota*)	24:5	20:12

Luke's narrative accentuates the connection between breaking bread, the first day of the week, and resurrection. Luke tells this story because on this particular first day of the week when the disciples were gathered to break bread they experienced firsthand a resurrection from the dead. The combination of these factors connects this narrative with Luke 24. The parallels between Acts 20 and Luke 24 (reflected in the chart below) indicate that Luke wants us to read Acts 20 in the light of Luke 24.

The Greek text of Acts 20:7 identifies the day of meeting as the "first day of the week." While Sabbath after Sabbath Paul was in the synagogues speaking to Jews (Acts 13:14, 44; 17:2; 18:4), when he encounters a Christian group, they are meeting on the first day of the week. It is uncertain whether this assumes a Jewish reckoning (sunset to sunset, so that Acts 20 = Saturday evening) or a Roman reckoning (sunrise to sunrise, so that Acts 20 = Sunday evening). Either way, they met on the first day of the week rather than on the Sabbath.

The "first day of the week" connects this text theologically with Luke 24. This is no mere temporal indicator or incidental reference. Rather, it is a theological marker. The first day of the week carries theological significance as the day of resurrection (an eighth day that symbolizes new creation—the eighth day is the next stage after the seven days of the first week), the birthday of the church (Pentecost; Lev. 23:9-21, 33-36), and the first day of creation itself. The first day of the week is rooted in the saving act of God in the gospel, the original act of God in creation, and the meaning of new creation. On that day the Spirit was poured out, a new community began, and new creation was inaugurated.

On the first day of the week, Jesus first appeared to his disciples, broke bread with them, and ate in their presence (Luke 24:13, 30, 33, 46). The first day of the week, then, as resurrection day and as the day on which Jesus ate with his disciples became the ordinary day when disciples would gather weekly to break bread together. While the Jerusalem church did this daily (sharing with travelers who came for Pentecost perhaps), daily observances were not uniform throughout the whole church. Troas appears to have practiced a weekly meal. The weekly observance became standard in the late first and mid-second centuries as indicated by the *Didache* (14:1) and Justin Martyr (*First Apology*, 46-47). Luke's language, in fact, may reflect a common way of expressing the Sunday gathering since the language of "gathering," "breaking bread," and "first day of the week" are commonly linked in early literature (1 Cor. 11:20; 16:1; *Didache* 14:1; Ignatius, *Ephesians* 20:2).

Given the links between Luke 24 and Acts 20, the "first day of the week" is no incidental reference. Both tell a resurrection story. Jesus emerges from the tomb "alive" and Eutychus goes home "alive." The resurrection of Eutyches is a concrete experience of victory for the church at Troas. When they gathered to break bread with the risen Eutychus, they ate with a visible example of resurrection hope. That supper was a celebration of hope and life. The congregation was greatly "comforted," which is what the contemporary church experiences when it breaks bread in the presence of the living Christ.

Some read this text as if there were two different breakings of bread. But the text does not say that they broke the bread in Acts 20:7, but only that they came together to break bread. They did not break bread until after Paul's homily and Eutychus's resurrection. (The text uses "Paul" as a synecdoche for the whole, that is, "he broke bread and ate" refers to the church for surely Paul did not eat alone!) They broke bread and ate when they returned to the upper room after the resurrection (sounds like Luke 24!). Just like the Jerusalem church they broke bread and ate food, praising God, and celebrating the resurrection. Breaking bread is a meal where the disciples eat together in the presence of the living Christ and, in this case, in the presence of the raised Eutychus.

The coordination of the first day of the week, breaking bread, and resurrection gives theological substance to a weekly celebration of the Lord's supper. Given that early Christians met every first day of the week (1 Cor. 16:1), and that they gathered to eat the Lord's supper (1 Cor. 11:20; Acts 20:7), there are good historical reasons for believing that Christians met every first day of the week in order to eat the Lord's supper. More importantly, there are theological reasons for affirming this due to the intersection of the first day of the week, resurrection, and breaking bread. The first day of the week is the day of remembrance, the day of our deliverance, because it is the day on which God raised Jesus from the dead and renewed Israel. It is the first day of new creation. It is a day of communal worship and celebration because of what God has done in the gospel, and the gospel is proclaimed in the Lord's supper. If the Lord's supper is a celebration of the resurrection, why omit the gift God has given us to celebrate it when we gather on the first day of the week to celebrate the resurrection?

Conclusion

Pentecost is Israel's new exodus. It inaugurates new creation as the Spirit is poured out on the new community. This initial outpouring is the first fruit of new creation itself. The descent of the Spirit is the fulfillment of the descent of the cloud and fire on the Tabernacle in Exodus 40. In fact, it is the renewal of God's rest within creation on the seventh day itself. Just as God rested in the temple, so now God rests within the church. What Israel received at Mt. Sinai was poured on the church at Mt. Zion. Moreover, this Spirit was poured out from the future. The presence of the Spirit is the presence of the future; it is the experience and promise of new creation.

Everyone first passed through the waters of the exodus and then experienced the filling, the tabernacling, of the Spirit in their lives. Passing through the waters, they devoted themselves to the teaching of the apostles and shared in the *koinonia* of the community as it began its wilderness pilgrimage. This *koinonia* was itself an expression of the common bond of the Spirit who united the community. More particularly, when they broke bread together, that is, when they ate a meal together hosted by the living Messiah, they experienced the joy of resurrection life. They ate with joy and generosity as they praised God for new life. They ate with hope as they re-experienced the victory of Jesus over death through eating together.

It is one of the great discontinuities between the meals in Luke and the contemporary church that joy is not the primary mood in which the contemporary supper is experienced. The church tends to eat the supper as if new creation has not yet begun, as if it is still Friday. But new creation began in the resurrection of Jesus and its first fruit was the outpouring of the Spirit at Pentecost. When the church eats, whatever day on which it might eat, it is always Sunday, the "eighth" day of creation—the first day of new creation.

Chapter 4

PAUL: From Death to Life with Jesus

Paul's Jewish worldview was immersed in the story of Jesus rather than in pagan Hellenism or mystery cults. His understanding of the sacraments is saturated with the backstory of Israel. In particular, it is shaped by Israel's exodus story.

This is clear from 1 Corinthians 10:1-4. Writing to a predominately Gentile congregation, Paul unites their experience of baptism and the Lord's supper with the story of Israel's crossing of the sea and their pilgrimage in the wilderness. Israel was "baptized into Moses in the cloud and in the sea," just as the church is baptized into the Messiah. Moreover, Israel ate the "same spiritual food" and drank the same "spiritual drink" that the church eats and drinks, that is, they were nourished by Christ.

The identity of Israel and the church—"our ancestors"—is rooted in their participation in the same story. They share Christ and they share the sacraments. What the crossing of the sea was to Israel typifies what baptism is to believers in Jesus. What eating and drinking were in the wilderness typifies what the Lord's supper is to the church. We are one people with one story.

From Death to Life Through Water

Baptismal texts abound in Paul. Sometimes Paul uses the term "wash" or "washing" to describe the function of baptism (1 Cor. 6:11; Eph. 5:26; Titus 3:5), but mostly he employs some form of the root which most translate as "baptize" or "baptism." More significantly, the varied contexts in which Paul employs baptismal motifs stress how important baptism is to Paul (Col. 2:12; Eph. 4:5; Gal. 3:27; 1 Cor. 1:13-17; 12:13). However, Paul's use of baptism in Romans 6:3-4 is his most compelling discussion because of how it is situated in the theological and narrative substructure of Romans 1-8.

A New Exodus Story

N. T. Wright suggests that Romans 3-8 follows the flow of Israel's story.[1]

The story begins with Abraham with whom God entered into covenant. God promised Abraham that his descendants would inherit a land and ultimately bless all nations. Eventually Jacob and his children migrated to Egypt where, some years later, Pharaoh enslaved them. After a number of years, God heard their lament as they pleaded for deliverance.

In response, God sent Moses to liberate them and lead them out of Egypt. The crossing of the sea was the climatic moment of salvation; it was the final defeat of the powers that enslaved them. God, then, led Israel through the wilderness to Mt. Sinai where they entered into covenant with God, and God gave them the Torah, the law. But the journey was not over. They wandered through the wilderness for another forty years as God led them by a pillar of cloud and fire. Eventually God led them into their inheritance, the land promised Abraham. Their exodus was a journey from slavery to freedom. They were no longer slaves but heirs.

Romans 1:18-3:20 indicts all humanity, both Jew and Gentile, with sin. Israel was just as faithless as the Gentiles since they failed to fulfill their commission as a light to the nations. Consequently the "whole world" was "held accountable to" God's righteousness. But God is faithful and did not leave the "whole world" under judgment. God appointed Jesus the Messiah, a descendent of Abraham through David, as a surrogate for Israel through whose faithfulness God would create anew (Rom. 3:21-31). Through the faithfulness of Jesus God renewed the promise to Abraham by restoring his family that now includes both Jews and Gentiles identified by faith in the Messiah.

This renewed family is, in fact, a new humanity. While old humanity, including Israel, was entrenched in sin and held in bondage to death itself, this new humanity is reconciled to God though the death of the Messiah and saved by his life (Rom. 5:1-11). Adam represents old humanity, but the Messiah represents new humanity. Sin and death reigned through Adam, but now grace and life reign through Jesus Christ. Human faithlessness, beginning in Adam and including Israel, brought condemnation, but the faithfulness of Jesus has set things right (Rom. 5:12-21).

The movement from old humanity to new humanity is a new exodus. Through baptism into the death and resurrection of the Messiah, believers cross the sea. Dying and rising with Christ, the old human is crucified and the new one is raised to a new life. *The Message* captures this image vividly (Rom. 6:3): "That is what happened in baptism. When we went under the water, we left the old country of sin behind; when we came up out of the water, we entered into the new country of grace—a new life in a new land." Our baptismal exodus ushers us into a new life because, through it, we participate in the death and resurrection of Christ that inaugurated new creation. Though we were designed to reign in the creation through Adam, sin terminated our reign and death obliterated it. But now, made anew in Christ, we reign in the creation through a righteousness that leads to eternal life. Ultimately, we will reign with Christ in our resurrected bodies on the new heaven and new earth, the redeemed creation—the new land (see also 2 Tim. 2:11-13 and Rev. 5:10).

Sin, however, is a problem. It has been a problem since Adam. After Israel crossed the sea, they were brought to Sinai and given the Torah. Just as Adam was given a command in the Garden and broke it, so Israel was given the Torah and they proved unfaithful. Israel was as guilty as Adam. Though the Torah was holy, just, and life-giving, it failed to give life to Israel because of sin. Israel did not escape the impact of

Adamic sin; they were not exempt from Adamic humanity. Instead, they followed Adam into faithlessness and were enslaved by the power of sin and death. Consequently, the Torah, rather than freeing them from their sin, highlighted it, and therefore Israel, like the rest of humanity, fell under condemnation (Rom. 7). They, like Adam from Eden, were exiled from their inheritance. Like the rest of humanity, they were enslaved to sin.

New humanity in Christ, however, is free from condemnation, liberated from bondage, and empowered to live out the righteous demands of the Torah because they live in the Spirit rather than in Adam (or, the flesh). Liberated from their slavery, new humanity lives in the power of the Spirit (Rom. 8:1-4). This life not only defeats sin, but also defeats death through the indwelling Spirit who will "give life to [our] mortal bodies" in the resurrection (Rom. 8:11). Given that we have received the Spirit of adoption, why would anyone want to return to living in fear under "a spirit of slavery" (Rom. 8:15)? Just as God was present with Israel through the pillar of cloud and fire as God led them through the wilderness, so now God is present within us to lead us through the wilderness of sin and death. The resolution to the power of sin in Adamic humanity is the presence of the Spirit.

As adopted children of God, people who cry "Abba, Father!" we are "heirs of God and joint heirs with Christ" (Rom. 8:16-17). But what is our inheritance? To what "land" are we headed as we presently wander through this wilderness? Through the Messiah we are heirs of Abraham who was promised that "he would inherit the world" (*cosmos*; Rom. 4:13). Paul extends the inheritance of Abraham beyond the land of Canaan. The whole world is the inheritance of the children of Abraham, which now include Jews and Gentiles. The children of God will inherit a new heaven and new earth.

This is the hope of new humanity. We groan, along with the whole cosmos, for the liberation of the creation from its "bondage to decay." The creation, due to Adamic sin, was "subjected to futility" and frustration in the hope that it would "be set free" from sin and death. The presence of the Spirit within the children of God is the "first fruits" of a harvest that will not only redeem our bodies from death through the resurrection, but also redeem the cosmos itself. This hope not only saves us but the creation itself. As children of God, we will inherit a new heaven and new earth where we will reign with Christ in our resurrected bodies. That is our promised land, our inheritance.

Israel was liberated from Egyptian bondage by crossing the sea and ultimately inherited the land of Canaan after years of wandering through the wilderness. In Christ, humanity is liberated from sin and death through baptism and empowered to life a new life through the Spirit as we wait for the liberation of our inheritance. Israel's exodus from Egyptian slavery to freedom, from homelessness to inheritance becomes humanity's exodus from death to life, from refugee status to a new home on the new heaven and new earth.

Reflections on Baptism

Romans 3-8 reinterprets Israel's exodus from Egyptian bondage as humanity's exodus from sin and death. The transitional moment in this story is the crossing of the sea, which is our baptism (Rom. 6). This gives a central place to baptism and invests it with redemptive meaning.

First, baptism marks our crossing from death to life. Baptism involves movement. We move from slavery to freedom, from death to life. Through baptism we cross the sea; we transition from old humanity to new humanity.

Paul accentuates this movement with the use of the preposition *eis* (into). *Eis* signifies movement, a transition from one place to another, and, given Paul's argument in Romans 3-8, a crossing over. We are (Rom. 6:3-4):

+ Baptized *into* Christ Jesus
+ Baptized *into* his death
+ Buried with him by baptism *into* death.

Baptism marks the moment when we transition from living outside of Christ to resting in Christ. "In Christ" is Paul's language for living in the reality of God's new creation. Union with Christ is Paul's way of talking about salvation. Baptism, for Paul, has soteriological significance. This is all the more evident as Paul connects baptism with the death and resurrection of Christ.

Our union with Christ means that his experience becomes our own. We are not only baptized into *his* death, but die with him in that baptism as we are plunged into *death* itself. Our old humanity is crucified and buried with Christ just as Christ's own Adamic humanity was crucified and buried. Jesus was raised as a new human, free from death itself. So, also, we are raised a new humanity free from the guilt and power of sin as well as from the dominion of death. Our union with the death of Christ is also our union with his resurrected life. We rise from the watery grave to live a new life.

Second, baptism is a means of grace. The action language of Romans 6 focuses on the moment of our union with Christ in baptism: buried, raised, united, crucified, and died. Baptism mediates this action as we die and rise *with* Christ. A single word highlights this mediation: *dia* (by or through). We are "buried with him by (*dia*) baptism into death."

Dia denotes instrumentality. Something happens *through* baptism. In traditional sacramental language this is identified as a "means of grace." God uses baptism as a means. In, with, and under the waters of baptism, God gives grace, or, more specifically in Romans 6, God unites us with the death and resurrection of Christ. This language excludes any kind of mere symbolism. Rather, it is an affirmation that something really happens in baptism, that is, *God does something.* Just as in Israel's crossing, so also in baptism, God liberates, redeems, and saves.

Third, baptism is freedom for holiness. The exodus language is powerfully accentuated in Romans 6 through the imagery of slavery. Our Adamic bodies were "enslaved to sin." But those who have died with Christ, and thus died to sin, are "freed from sin." But this is no mere liberation from the guilt of sin. Rather, it is liberation from the power of sin so that we might live to God. Our baptism means that, having died to sin, sin will have no more "dominion" over us. We are freed from the slavery of sin so that we might use our freedom for holiness and "present" ourselves "to God as instruments of righteousness." Freed from the bondage of the Adamic humanity, our new humanity bears the fruit of holiness through the power of the Spirit.

Fourth, baptism is the promise of life with Christ. Just as Christ was raised never to die again because "death no longer has dominion over him," so those united to Christ will participate in his resurrection and dominion over death. For "if we have died with Christ," Paul writes, "we believe that we will also live with him" (Rom. 6:8). This is the hope of "eternal life." While many think of "eternal life" as living in heaven with God forever, Paul believes it is the redemption of our bodies, liberated from the bondage of decay.

Baptism affirms the redemption of creation because it testifies to the future of our bodies. The resurrection of our bodies is our liberation from the bondage of death, and the whole creation will participate in our glorious freedom. Our baptism, then, has cosmic meaning; it bears witness to the glorious future of creation itself. *Baptism is a cosmic testimony!*

Baptism, in Romans 6, is the story of a new exodus moment. We have entered a new country. We have moved from living under the slavery of our Adamic humanity to the freedom of the new humanity rooted in the death and resurrection of Jesus the Messiah. We are no longer enslaved to sin but free to live in the Spirit. Death no longer has dominion over us but we live in the hope of eternal life. Baptism not only marks this new exodus, but it mediates to us the freedom, power, and hope of life.

Food and Drink in the Wilderness

The exodus ushered Israel into the wilderness. God led them to Sinai and then subsequently to the promised land, their inheritance. That journey through the wilderness lasted forty years.

Paul locates the church in a similar circumstance (1 Cor. 10:1-22). Both Israel and the church pass through the waters into the wilderness. Both Israel and the church are refugees in the wilderness nourished by the "same spiritual food" and "spiritual drink." Both are homeless but bound for the promised land. Israel received their inheritance when they crossed the Jordan River, and the church will receive its inheritance when God renews the creation.

However, the wilderness is filled with danger. Israel's wilderness experience was designed to humble and test them so that God would know what was in their hearts (Deut. 8:1-11). In the same way, the church's wilderness pilgrimage is designed to humble and test. This imagery is powerfully played out in the Apocalypse where the church in the wilderness, though protected and nourished, is also tested (Rev. 2:10; 12:6, 14).

Israel's wilderness trek is an example for the church. God "was not pleased with most of them, and struck them down in the wilderness." Israel encountered the dangers of idolatry and immorality. What will the church do when it encounters the same dangers in their journey toward the promised land? How will the church fare when it, too, is tested in the wilderness?

At Which Table Do We Eat? (1 Corinthians 10)

While Israel ate and drank the "same spiritual" nourishment that the church does, they also ate and drink at idolatrous tables. At Sinai, in the presence of a golden calf, Israel "sat down to eat and drink, and they rose up to play." Quoting Exodus 32:6, Paul contrasts their spiritual eating and drinking with their idolatrous eating and drinking, which included sexual immorality. Israel attempted to eat at two tables—the table of the Lord and the table of idols. God's covenant people were disloyal. Consequently, they were "struck down in the wilderness." Let this be a lesson, Paul writes, for the church.

Sacramental experiences—baptism and the Lord's supper—do not guarantee redemption. Salvation is experienced through baptism and the Lord's supper, but these moments also commit believers to the covenant. They call believers to an ethical lifestyle that imitates the Lord. Worship without ethics has always been unacceptable, and no baptism or table can "save" those who arrogantly violate their covenantal commitments.

At the same time, those who ate the sacrifices in Israel participated in the altar. In other words, those who sat at table to eat the sacrificial meat enjoyed the benefits of the altar. The key benefit is the ability, as we saw in Exodus 24:9-11, to see or experience God's presence, or to eat "before the LORD" (Deut. 27:7). While the meal obligated those who ate and drank to keep the covenant, it was also a means by which they communed with God. This is also true of the Lord's table.

The breaking of bread and the blessing of the cup are a communion or participation in the body and blood of Christ (1 Cor. 10:16). We commune with the altar (the cross). In other words, we commune with God through eating and drinking at the Lord's table because we share in the benefits of the altar.

To fellowship the altar is to enjoy and experience its atoning benefits. Just as the altar enabled Israel to sit at table with God, so the cross enables Christians to sit at the table. Thus, eating and drinking at the table of the Lord enjoys the reconciliation that the altar effected between God and humanity.

The communion, however, is not simply between God and those at the table. It is also the communion of the body of Christ itself—a horizontal fellowship among those who sit at the table. Though many members, the church is one because it shares the one bread and one cup of the table. When the church eats and drinks, it shares the same body and blood. By visibly eating and drinking together, the church displays and experiences the unity of the body in Christ.

The covenant nature of the Lord's supper means that we enjoy God's presence at the table with us because of God's gracious initiative at the altar, and we renew our covenantal commitment to God and to each other through eating and drinking. The Lord's supper is a gracious moment of communion and rededication. God renews covenant with us and we renew covenant with God. The Lord's table is a meal where we bind ourselves to God and to each other.

Whenever we eat and drink, we must ask at whose table do we sit? If we sit at the Lord's table, we cannot sit at another. The table of the Lord is a singular commitment and admits no other lordship in our lives. To eat and drink at the table of the Lord is to confess that we are disciples of Jesus and follow no other.

Eating Worthy of the Gospel (1 Corinthians 11)
Paul was not happy with how the Corinthians practiced the

Lord's supper. They had radically distorted its meaning. The form of their supper subverted the gospel that the supper proclaims. It is important, then, to identify the nature of the form that rendered the Corinthian proclamation of the gospel null and void.

Meeting in the home of one of the wealthier members of the congregation, the supper (*deipnon*, the evening meal) was apparently conducted in Greco-Roman style. Greco-Roman meals were occasions of social stratification, drunkenness, and disorderliness. Meals were a moment when social standing played into who sat where, when one ate, and how much and what they were served.

This scenario emerged at Corinth's meal (1 Cor. 11:17-22). The rich divided themselves from the poor so that they ate and drank without them. The poor, perhaps slaves or lower class workers, arrived later when the food and drink were gone. The poor, then, went hungry while the rich were well-fed and some of them drunk. Instead of transforming Greco-Roman meals by the values of the gospel, the Lord's supper was transformed into a Greco-Roman meal.

Taking pride in their wealth and social status, some Corinthians did not wait for others to arrive. They proceeded with their meal without the whole church present. The Corinthians exhibited a spiritual arrogance by dividing the body into the very socio-economic strata that the gospel intended to obliterate. Consequently, the Corinthians failed to appreciate the meaning of the gospel, which intends to unite diverse groups, transcend cultural and fallen distinctions, and testify to the common bond of the body of Christ. The

Corinthians drank judgment upon themselves because they denied the gospel by the way in which they conducted what was supposed to be the Lord's supper. Otherwise, like Israel at Sinai, the church returns to Egypt.

As a corrective to their practices, Paul points his readers to the Last Supper (1 Cor. 11:23-26). The practice of the Lord's supper must be shaped by Jesus' original intent. This is the *Lord's* supper, not their own. Consequently, the practice of the supper must be shaped by the gospel rather than by Greco-Roman culture.

Paul's recollection of the Last Supper does not exclude a meal but rather refocuses it. The Lord's meal must be shaped by the values of the cross, that is, by the self-emptying act of Jesus whose body and blood was given for us. In the midst of an evening meal—a *deipnon*—we should experience the good news that Jesus gave himself for us so that we might sit at the table as the one body of Christ. As the body of Christ, we are called to give ourselves to each other. The table becomes a moment of self-emptying that imitates the self-giving of Jesus. Consequently, Greco-Roman values, which deny the gospel, must not shape the form and meaning of the table. The cross must shape its form and meaning.

This does not mean that the table becomes an altar. Rather, the table embodies the life given at the cross. In this sense the table proclaims the "Lord's death." It proclaims good news and how the Lord's death has broken down all social, racial, and gender barriers. It proclaims the unity of the body of Christ at the table of the Lord. Proclaiming the death of Christ is the good news that the gospel redeems all sinful structures. But when the table reintroduces those sinful structures—as it did at Corinth—it denies the gospel.

Despite their negative habits, Paul still wants them to eat together. Instead of discarding the meal, he tells them to wait for each other. If they are so hungry that they cannot wait, then they should eat something at home before they come to the assembly. The solution is simple: wait and if you cannot, then eat something at home to hold you over till everyone arrives. The main point is that the church should eat together as a community rather than divided by socio-economic structures.

Rather than divided among ourselves, we must "discern the body" when we eat. This phrase has been the subject of considerable controversy. Some argue that it means to "discern" the body (flesh) of Christ, the physical substance, in the bread. Some argue that it refers to the subjective state of worshippers as they introspectively discern the seriousness of their act of communion and reflect on the meaning of the death of Christ. Indeed, some believe that one must exclusively think about the cross in order to worthily discern the body of Christ. These perspectives understand the word "body" to refer to the physical body of Jesus that suffered on the cross.

However, there is another, and preferable, understanding. To "discern the body" means to discern the church as a community. This points us to the communal meaning of the Lord's supper. To discern the body is to partake of the supper in a way that bears witness not only to the unity of the body of Christ (church) but also to the fellowship of that body which transcends all social and economic barriers. Thus, Paul's statement is directly linked to the specific problem in the Corinthian assembly. The problem is not that the Corinthians did not meditate on the cross, but that they did not embody the cross in a communal way at the table.

One indicator that Paul is talking about the church rather than the physical body of Christ is his language. When Paul is thinking about communing with the body and blood of Christ, he uses both "body and blood" as in 1 Corinthians 10:16 and 11:27. However, in 1 Corinthians 11:29, as in 1 Corinthians 10:17, he only refers to the "body." Just as in 1 Corinthians 10:16-17, Paul subtly shifts from "body and blood" (Jesus) to "body" (the church). The two are intimately connected because it is the body and blood of Christ that grounds the church as a community (the body of Christ). The common bond of the church is the body and blood of Christ. When the church eats and drinks the body and blood of Christ, it does so as the body of Christ (the church). The altar and the table are connected. The altar grounds and enables the table just as the body and blood of Christ grounds and establishes the church as God's one people. At the table, then, we must discern the unity and community of this body in order to eat and drink worthily.

Consequently, to eat and drink worthily is not about private introspection, but public action. Paul is not stipulating a kind of meditative silence on the cross of Christ or an introspective assessment of our relative holiness. On the contrary, to eat in an "unworthy manner," in this context, is to eat in a divisive manner. The church must examine itself regarding the manner in which the supper is conducted. There may be many ways in which to eat the supper unworthily (e.g., 1 Cor. 10:18-21, eating with dual commitment), but the specific unworthiness in 1 Corinthians 11 is a communal problem, not an individual one. The church eats worthily when it eats as a united community embodying the values for which Christ died.

When the church fails to embody those values, then it denies the gospel. When it denies the gospel, then it condemns itself as it eats and drinks judgment upon itself. The Lord's table is a serious moment. It is not serious because it is quiet time or because it functions as penance. Rather, it is serious because it bears witness to the gospel. Judgment comes to those who deny the gospel. That is not about a momentary lapse of focused concentration on the cross. It is about embodying the gospel as a community when the church comes together to eat and drink.

Conclusion

The story of Israel continues in the church. Little wonder, then, they share similar experiences. Both passed through the waters, and both journeyed in the wilderness anticipating their inheritance. They were both baptized into a new community, a new country. They were both nourished by the same spiritual food and drink.

The critical difference, however, is that church plays out Israel's story at a cosmic level. While Israel crossed the sea to escape Egyptian slavery, humanity passes through the waters to escape the bondage of sin and death. While Israel was sustained by God's nourishment and presence in the wilderness, the church is nourished by new creation life because of the death and resurrection of the Messiah. While Israel inherited the land of Canaan, the renewed people of God will inherit the cosmos in a new heaven and new earth.

Passing through the waters, we become part of a new humanity. Pilgrimaging through the wilderness, we are led by Spirit, nourished by Christ, and united at the table as we await our inheritance.

Chapter 5

NEW CREATION: A Promised Future Already Present

The term "eschatology," like "sacrament," is often regarded as a cerebral term. Fair enough, but it is helpful shorthand for something deeply embedded in the story of God.

Creation's grand purpose, which was begun on the first day, finds its ultimate end in the eschaton. But I do not mean "end" in the sense of being finished with creation. Rather, the "end" of creation is its goal—the destination toward which creation was always headed. While creation reveals God's intent, the eschaton reveals God's goal.

Creation gives us our identity (image of God), our vocation (to partner with God), and defines our mission. It establishes community and relationship—with God, each other, and the rest of creation. The eschaton brings to fulfillment all that God intended in creation. It actualizes the fullness of the kingdom of God that fills the whole earth with justice, peace, and righteousness. It is community and communion in the new creation.

But eschatology is not simply futuristic. Rather, new creation is revealed in and through the Christ Event. The incarnation, ministry, death, resurrection, and ascension of Jesus declare both the intent and goal of God. The risen Messiah is the living presence of God embodying the reality that God always intended for humanity and what God will ultimately actualize in the eternal kingdom on the new heaven and new earth.

The church, initiated into the new creation through baptism and nourished by the living Christ through the Lord's supper, is called to embody the life and ministry of Jesus in the present. Through the sacraments the church, by the power of the Spirit, is invigorated and refreshed with new life, eschatological life. Eschatology, then, is not only future; it is the air that the church breathes, even now.

Understanding Eschatology

Too often "eschatology" (the study of the last things or last days) is focused on millennial debates (versions of postmillennialism, premillennialism, realized millennialism) and the eternal destiny of human beings (heaven or hell). Some ignore the debates because they seem irrelevant (God is going to do what God is going to do) while others are consumed by them (check the web!).

Eschatology, however, is not so much about what happens last—and the order in which it happens—as much as it is about *the future that is already at work.*

Christology: The New Creation has Begun

The kingdom of God is already present within the old age. The old age and the new age overlap as God moves creation from old to new through a redemptive transformation. The church, indwelt by the Spirit of God, participates in that process—we are increasingly changed from one form of glory to another. Ultimately, the whole creation will share in that glory.

New creation began with the Christ Event—the incarnation, ministry, death, resurrection, and ascension of Jesus the Messiah. In one sense, Christology is eschatology. The resurrection, for example, gave birth to a new humanity that belongs to the new heaven and new earth; Jesus is the firstborn from the dead. But we might also think about the death of Jesus as eschatological as well. His death was, in some sense, the experience of second death or an eschatological death for our sakes. Jesus experienced death for us and transformed death through the resurrection. Also, the ministry of Jesus proclaimed the good news of the kingdom, and his kingdom works demonstrated the presence of the future. The future—diseases healed, demons expelled, death reversed—broke into the present through the ministry of Jesus. Jesus' healing ministry reversed creation's curse as it heralded the coming kingdom. Even the incarnation is eschatological as it is the ultimate union of God and humanity.

The ascension of the Messiah to the Davidic throne after the resurrection is the climactic eschatological event—though often neglected. Raised from the dead, Christ ascended to the right of the Father to sit and reign in the heavenlies (Eph. 1:19). From there he pours out the Spirit upon the people of God, rules the creation as he brings its chaos and death into subjection, and intercedes for his people. Most significantly, as the new human—the resurrected Messiah—he lives in a form that unites heaven and earth. His glorious humanity (immortal body and soul) lives in the presence of God, and one day he will live in the new Jerusalem upon a new earth. The Messianic reign of Jesus is the reign of new humanity preparing a new Jerusalem for a new heaven and earth.

Resurrection: The Christian Hope
Death is the epitome of the broken world; it is the last enemy (1 Cor. 15:26). This hated enemy enslaves humanity as it fosters doubt and fear. The Christian hope is not an immortal soul living in heaven but an immortal humanity (body and soul) living upon the new earth.

If Jesus, as the resurrected new human, is the first fruits, the redeemed people of God are the harvest of new humanity (1 Cor. 15:20-23). The first fruits were the initial part of the annual crops offered to God in acknowledgement of God's blessing. This grateful offering trusted that God would bring the rest of the harvest to fruition.

The resurrection of Jesus and the resurrection of believers are one; they belong to the same harvest. The resurrection of Jesus and that of believers belong to the same continuum. They are a single event in redemptive history though they are now separated by almost two thousand years. The resurrection of Jesus is proleptic, that is, it is the presence of the future, the presence of new creation, within the old creation. The resurrection of Jesus, though a present reality, belongs to the future and assures our future. The resurrection of Jesus, then, is the pledge of a future harvest, a preview of coming attractions.

Jesus is first—the firstborn from the dead. But he is more—he is the pattern. We will bear the image of the heavenly human, the second Adam, just as we now bear the image of the first Adam. Christ is the new humanity. We will participate in his new humanity; our bodies will be like his (1 Cor. 15:49; Phil. 3:21).

The resurrection of our new humanity, patterned after and grounded in the resurrection of Jesus, is the Christian hope. The contrast between our present Adamic existence within this old creation and our future Christic existence in the new creation is the contrast between mortal and immortal, between dishonor and glory, between weakness and power, and between "natural" and "spiritual" (1 Cor. 15:42-44).

The "natural" (literally, "soulish") body is a material substance animated by earthly resources where "flesh and blood" is nourished by created life. The "spiritual" body is a material substance animated by heavenly resources as the Holy Spirit sustains new humanity. New humanity, in both body and soul, lives by the power of the Spirit of God.

New Heavens and New Earth: The Divine Goal

Where will this Spirit-animated material body live? To answer I return to God's grand purpose in creation.

God rests in, delights in, cares for, and rejoices over the creation. God intends to redeem it rather than annihilate it, just as God intends to redeem humanity (body and soul). The creation, like humanity, groans for redemption and hopes for a glorious liberation alongside the children of God (Rom. 8:18-24). The present creation, frustrated by chaos and sin, hopes for an exodus that will renew it.

This is what the prophets expected—the restoration or regeneration of all things (Acts 3:21). Isaiah gives us the language of "new heavens and new earth" (Isa. 65:17; 66:22). Both Peter (2 Pet. 3:13) and John (Rev. 21:1-4) use it to describe the final goal of God's redemptive work.

In Revelation, John sees the new Jerusalem descend out of the heavenly throne room onto the new earth. In effect, heaven comes to earth; heaven and earth become one. God comes to dwell in the new Jerusalem—"the Lord God Almighty and the Lamb are its temple" (Rev. 21:22). Just as in Eden when God rested and dwelt upon the earth, so when the grand purpose of God is finished God will again rest and dwell upon the earth.

The old age, at that point, will have passed away. Death, mourning, pain, and the curse will be no more (Rev. 21:4; 22:3). The first order, including our Adamic bodies, will pass away and the new creation, with humanity bearing the image of the resurrected Messiah, will fully emerge. The glory of God will fill the earth, and the people of God will see the face of God.

Sacraments, Creation and New Creation

So, what does eschatology have to do with sacramental theology? Practically everything! The sacraments are where the old creation meets the new.

Created materiality is good; indeed, it is very good. It is delightful and wondrous. God created the world as a temple in which to dwell, a place where God and humanity would enjoy each other, delight in the wonder of the cosmos, care for it, and rest within it. We participate in the communion of God's life through materiality. Creation is not an addendum or a secondary reality but a means by which humanity experiences God.

But, alas, creation is now broken. It is still good, but broken. It is enslaved, infected with unruly chaos and pervasive sin. Nevertheless, creation still serves its function. We still experience God through creation as, for example, when we enjoy the beauty of a sunset. We experience God in its little things as well as in its majestic views. Yet, creation is frustrated. It is filled with pain, tragedy, and death. Like the cosmos itself, we are frustrated and yearn for liberation.

Despite its brokenness, God affirmed the goodness of creation through the Christ Event that inaugurated new humanity. The Son is new creation, the second Adam, the new human. Because of the Messiah's work, *the sacraments are a place where the new creation breaks into the old one.* They are moments where God offers us a taste of new creation.

Baptism is water but more than water. It is not a "regular" dip in water. We may experience God in the shower, through a long hot bath, or by a swim in the ocean. Old creation is still good and still mediates God's presence. But baptism is more.

Baptism is the experience of new creation. The water of the old creation becomes a means by which we experience the new. It is still water—created materiality is not annihilated—but it is also a participation in the reality of the new creation through our union with Christ. Through baptism we participate in the death and resurrection of Jesus. We rise from the watery grave to live as new creatures. Baptism is a new creation bath that does not annihilate materiality or creation. Rather, it ushers us, by the Spirit, into the heavenlies where we are seated with Christ at the right hand of God (Eph. 2:6). In baptism, we experience our resurrection as if it has already happened. Death has no claim upon us because we have been baptized. We are new creatures in Christ.

The Lord's supper is bread and wine, but more than bread and wine. It is not a "regular" meal. We may experience God through any meal, whether it is the nightly family meal, the church potluck, or the annual Thanksgiving dinner. Old creation is still good and still mediates God's presence. But the Lord's supper is more.

The Lord's supper is the experience of new creation. The bread and wine of the old creation become means by which we experience the new. It is still bread and wine—created materiality is not annihilated—but it is also a participation in the reality of the new creation through the presence of Christ. Whether we think of that presence in the bread, through the bread, or at the table is inconsequential to my point. The Eucharistic meal is a new creation meal that does not annihilate creation. Rather, it transforms it, liberates it, and brings it to its goal. In the supper, the living Christ nourishes us. We are nourished by the life of the new creation.

Baptism and the Lord's supper are sacred moments. They are places, by the promise of God, where God meets us in this old, frustrated creation that we might experience—taste, get a glimpse of—new creation. They are moments of both authentic participation in the new creation as well as anticipations of its coming fullness. Through the sacraments, God communes with us and assures us that one day the frustrations of creation will pass away and all creation will be liberated and renewed.

We must only have the eyes of faith to see it and experience it. God is present even when we don't realize it. By faith we embrace these sacred moments and lean into the future. By faith, we experience grace through baptism and are nourished by the table.

This is why I love the sacraments—they are God's gifts through which we experience new creation and anticipate the new heaven and new earth. They are injections of hope in a broken world, previews of coming attractions, and proleptic experiences of what is to come.

Old creation is good, but new creation is better.

Eschatological Horizons in Baptism and the Lord's Supper

Baptism is our initiation into new creation life, and we are nourished in that new life by the Lord's meal.

Baptism as Eschatological Initiation

First, through baptism God makes us alive with, raises us up with, and seats us with Christ in the heavenlies (Eph. 2:4-7; Col. 2:11-13). Paul stresses the effect of God's gracious love and mercy with three verbs in Ephesians 2:5-6: *made alive together, raised together,* and *seated together.* This movement—coming to life, rising, and being seated—is shared *with Christ.* God is the subject of these verbs; they are divine acts. The movement from death to exaltation in the experience of Jesus the Messiah becomes our experience as well. Just as Jesus was raised from the dead and enthroned at the right hand of God, so we are made alive, raised, and seated with him.

We are seated with Jesus "in the heavenly places." In other words, we are present in the heavenly throne room with Christ. Just as Jesus began the new creation through resurrection and enthronement, so we are initiated into new creation by being raised and seated with Christ in the heavenlies. We are new creatures—"created in Christ Jesus" (Eph. 2:10)—seated in the new creation, inhabiting the heavenlies. It is little wonder, then, that Paul thinks that our "citizenship is in heaven" (Phil 3:21) because this is where we are already enthroned with Christ. Dead in our sins, we "followed the ruler of the power of the air" and "lived in the passions of our flesh" (Eph. 2:2-3), but now raised and seated with Christ, we live by a different power and in different passions.

But where is baptism in this text? Though Ephesians 2 does not specifically mention baptism, "made alive" and "raised with" are baptismal phrases. Paul only uses this language in Ephesians 2:5-6, Colossians 3:12-13, and Colossians 3:1.

Ephesians 2:5-6	Colossians 3:12-13
even when we were dead through our trespasses, *made us alive together with Christ*—by grace you have been saved—and *raised us up with him* and seated us with him in the heavenly places in Christ Jesus...	having been buried with him in baptism, in which you were also *raised with him* through faith in the powerful working of God, who raised him from the dead. And you, who were dead in your trespasses and the uncircumcision of your flesh, God *made alive together with him*, having forgiven us all our trespasses...

Colossians 3:1 calls those who "have been raised with Christ" to "seek" what is "above, where Christ is, seated at the right

hand of God." The movement of Christ from resurrection to exaltation in Colossians 2-3 is the same as Ephesians 2, and Colossians 2 locates this movement "in baptism." Those who "have been raised with Christ" should embrace the life from "above" rather than from the "earth." In other words, we live in the heavenlies with Christ. Consequently, baptized people—those who have been made alive and raised with Christ—live as though heaven has come to earth.

Baptized people—those united with Christ in his death, resurrection, and exaltation—live by the values that permeate the heavenlies, the new creation. Baptized people are new creation people. Enthroned with Christ, we are co-rulers of the new creation just as humanity was created to co-rule the original creation in Genesis 1.

Second, through baptism we are united with the body of Christ, God's new creation (Gal. 3:26-4:6; 1 Cor. 12:12-13). As noted in Chapters One and Four, Paul sees baptism through the lens of the exodus. Just as Israel was baptized in the cloud and sea, so believers pass through the waters in their own exodus. They are freed from the guilt and bondage of sin, and they are united with the body of Christ in a new community.

This new community emerges out of God's history with Israel. God's faithfulness to Israel through Jesus the Messiah renewed Israel as a new creation among the peoples of the earth. However, this Israel is neither ethnic nor nationalistic in character. It transcends the boundary markers of the Torah. Neither circumcision nor uncircumcision matters any longer; what is important is "new creation" (Gal. 6:15).

New creation subverts all structures within human history that divide, exclude, or oppress people. New creation heals the brokenness of the old. It opposes the use of circumcision as a boundary marker for God's eschatological people. It opposes the role of slavery in human economics. It opposes oppressive power relationships that have distorted male-female relations. New creation is the renewal of God's original vision for creation. Paul underscores this point in Galatians 3:28 when he echoes Genesis 1:27: "male or female." God's intent in creation is realized in God's new creation.

We are not only baptized into a new community but into a new world. The old rules no longer apply. We have moved from the kingdom of Satan into the kingdom of God's Son. We no longer live according to the patterns of broken cultural mores. Rather, we lean into the future; we imagine, through Scripture and with the help of the Holy Spirit, the world God envisions. As God's new creation, we live as if the kingdom of God has fully come into the world even as we wait for its ultimate arrival.

Through faith, our baptism effects and confesses the newness and oneness of the body of Christ. Our baptism makes a claim upon us—it unites us with the kingdom of God. It affirms an allegiance that transcends all other ethnic, nationalistic, or social allegiances. We are members of the body of Christ, and this shapes every other value. This is our identity, our citizenship. We are part of God's new creation where every ethnicity, nation, and language lives in peace and justice.

Moreover, every ethnicity, nation, and language within this new creation is an heir of the Abrahamic promise and calls the God of Israel "Abba" through the Spirit (Gal. 4:6). Baptized in the Spirit and having drunk in the Spirit, the Spirit defines, empowers, and transforms the body of Christ as new creation. Just as the physical body of Jesus was raised from the dead in the power of the Spirit, so we are raised with Christ in baptism by that same power. The Spirit creates the new community and grounds its status before the Father. The presence of the eschatological Spirit in the community of God unites us in one new creation.

God tasked humanity with filling the earth and inhabiting the whole earth so that the glory of God might fill it. When the earth became full of violence and immorality, God promised to multiply Abraham's seed and make him an heir of the cosmos (Rom. 4:13). Israel was told to multiply and fill the land it was given so that the nations might know Yahweh. Through Abraham's seed the whole earth would come to know God, and in Abraham's seed both Jew and Greek, slave and free, male and female, become heirs of the cosmos. The one body of Christ will inherit the earth as the heirs of Abraham. God's new humanity will inhabit a new heaven and new earth.

Baptism initiates us into the life and future of the new creation.

The Lord's Supper as Eschatological Meal

The eschatological horizon reminds us that the root metaphor of the Lord's supper is neither tomb nor altar, but table. At this meal, we see social dimensions like hospitality and table fellowship in a new light as we eat together and are nourished in the Lord's presence.

The link between the supper and the second coming of Christ is acknowledged by all in light of 1 Corinthians 11:26. However this link is sometimes reduced to a temporal terminus when the supper will end, a promised fact, or a pledge of the future. In each of these, the eschatology is wholly future. They emphasize the "not-yetness" of the eschaton.

This futurist theology is often paired with memorialism. When the eschatological dimension of the table is neglected, the supper is easily reduced to a singular purpose such as remembering the death of Christ. There is no eschatological dynamic in the present but only an absent Christ whose return we await through memory. This lack of eschatological "alreadiness" engenders a solemn and funerary atmosphere that is more consistent with the metaphor of an altar than a table.

The table metaphor, however, points to an eschatological horizon in at least two ways: who is *at the table* and the food *on the table*.

First, Jesus is the living host of the table. Through the Lord's supper disciples experience the eschatological joy of the risen Christ as he hosts our communal meal in a proleptic experience of the future Messianic banquet. The living Christ is present at the table, seated with his welcome guests, eating and drinking with them, and providing the meal as a gracious gift.

Several key phrases in the Gospel accounts of the Last Supper ground this point. Luke 22:16-17 announces Jesus' intent to eat and drink again when the Passover meal finds its fulfillment in the kingdom of God. Jesus is no mere spectator, and neither is he merely the content of the meal. Rather, he is an active participant who eats and drinks at the table.

The continuity between the ministry tables (Luke 9), the Last Supper (Luke 22), and post-resurrection meals (Luke 24) is the presence of the living Christ in the breaking of the bread. "The eschatological prospect held out by Jesus at the Last Supper," Geoffrey Wainwright writes, "did not have to await the church's eucharist for its fulfillment, let alone remain unfulfilled until a coming of the kingdom which has even yet not occurred, but was *already fulfilled in the meals which Jesus took with His disciples immediately after his resurrection.*"[1] The continuity between the Gospel of Luke and the breaking of bread in Acts is the eschatological reality of the resurrected Jesus. *It is the continuation of the post-resurrection meals.* "The Last Supper and those resurrection appearances," T. F. Torrance writes, "belong together in one sacramental whole. Though Jesus has withdrawn His visible presence from us, there is such an intervention by the risen Lord as the invisible reality behind each celebration of the Lord's Supper. Jesus Christ is as really present in the Eucharist as He was on that Easter day to His disciples."[2]

More explicitly, in Matthew's account, Jesus states his expectation that when he drinks the cup anew in the kingdom of God he will do so—as he says to his disciples—"with *(meta)* you" (26:29) just as earlier Jesus had stated his intent "to keep the Passover . . . with *(meta)* my disciples" (26:18). In Matthew this is significant language as he begins his gospel with "Immanuel" which means "God with *(meta)* us" (1:23) and ends his gospel with the promise that the risen Lord would always be "with *(meta)* you" (28:20).

This language is pregnant with meaning. Jesus is with us at the table. This is about presence, but more than that. It is about participation, but even more. It is about a shared meal—mutuality, reciprocity, and an experience of active communion with the living Christ.

At the table, Jesus hosts, eats and drinks, communes, shares, and loves. God is with us in the human, risen Christ, and we eat at God's table in God's kingdom. This is a gracious gift and a demonstration of God's love. We—undeserving, unworthy—eat with God. We—unexpectedly, wondrously, joyfully—eat with Jesus.

Why, then, does sadness dominate our tables in our assemblies? Why can we not eat and drink with joy since we eat and drink with the living Christ? Jesus is at the table!

When I visualize the risen Christ at the table, a pleasant smile appears on my face. Sometimes it seems to annoy those sitting around me. But I smile because I am already at the eschatological table with Jesus . . . and with Joshua (my deceased son), Dad, Sheila (my deceased wife), and with all the saints.

The eschatological dimension of the Lord's supper, therefore, is not simply a proclamation of a future fact, nor is it merely the promise of a future reality. It is the experience of that future in the present through the Spirit who unites us with the living Christ in the throne room of God. Jesus invites us to his table even now, and we participate in the eschatological banquet even now. We already sit at the table of the king in his kingdom.

Second, we feed on the living Christ at the table. I have sometimes heard it said that the supper should be reverent and solemn because "the dead body of Jesus is on the table." No doubt they are thinking about Jesus as a sacrificial victim. "This is my body which is given for you" or "This is my blood which is poured out for many." This connects the table to the cross since Jesus gave his body on the cross and poured out his blood at the cross. We eat the sacrificial victim just as Israel ate the Passover lamb.

However, there is something amiss here. Is it the "dead body of Jesus" on the table? I think not. Do we eat the dead body of Christ? I think not. For one thing, Jesus is not dead but alive.

My point is not about whether it is a literal body/blood or not, but what is the body/blood offered to us in our eating and drinking? Are we nourished in the supper by the dead body of Jesus (perhaps only its mere memory) or by the living, resurrected body of Christ?

Here John 6 helps us. Jesus uses strong, even offensive, language. Unless we eat his flesh and drink his blood, he says, we will not have eternal life. In the context of John 6, the flesh and blood of Jesus is not understood as lifeless food but as living nourishment. It is the living flesh and blood of Jesus—it is the living Christ—that nourishes us. To eat the flesh of Jesus and to drink his blood is to intake life, an eternal life. It is to experience eschatological life, the life of the resurrected Jesus.

Jesus tells those who are seeking loaves that such food only satisfies for a moment but the Son of Man gives "food that endures to eternal life" (John 6:27). Indeed, the Son of Man is himself the living bread of a new Passover meal. He is the "bread of life" (John 6:35). This eternal life is present but also eschatological, that is, it is the resurrection life of the last day (John 6:40).

Jesus then becomes more specific about the nature of this living food that gives eternal life. One must, Jesus says, "eat the flesh of the Son of Man and drink his blood" in order to have life (John 6:53). Flesh and blood clearly point to the humanity of the Son of Man but the "eternal life" (John 6:54) that comes through eating and drinking points us to the heavenly (eschatological) nature of the Son of Man. Eating and drinking are means by which, Jesus says, one "remains in me, and I in him" (John 6:56). It is a spiritual union, an intimacy that is made possible by the sacrifice of the Passover Lamb and by feeding on that sacrifice.

"Eating flesh" was too much for some disciples. They grumbled about his meaning. This feeding, however, is rooted in the exalted nature of the Son of Man whom they will "see . . . ascend to where he was before" (John 6:62). His return to heaven—the ascension—empowers the Spirit to give life even when flesh per se "counts for nothing" (John 6:63). The exalted, ascended Son of Man gives life by the power of the Spirit to his disciples through eating his flesh and drinking his blood.

Resurrection language is foundational for Jesus' meaning in John 6. Whoever believes in the Son has eternal life, and "I will raise him up on the last day" (John 6:40). Jesus is the living bread of life, and those who eat enjoy eternal life. It is the "flesh and blood" of the eschatological, resurrected Son of Man that is given to us for eating and drinking. We don't eat dead but living flesh. We don't drink dried up blood but living blood. This is not the flesh and blood of the Adamic body, but the life-giving body of the heavenly human, Jesus Christ.

We eat his flesh and drink his blood at the table as the Holy Spirit presents to us the living Son of Man. While flesh means nothing, the Spirit gives eternal life through eating and drinking. The realistic language upsets many—as it did disciples at the time it was spoken—but it points to the reality of a communion between Christ and believers through the Spirit. By the Spirit we enjoy not only the forgiveness that the death of Jesus produced for us but we also enjoy the eternal life that is grounded in the resurrection and ascension of the Son of Man. We feed on the living Christ who fills us with his life, the life of new creation. When we eat and drink the life of the Son of Man at his table we enjoy, even now, the new, abundant life he brings, and we anticipate the fullness of that life in the coming resurrection.

Like John Calvin, I envision it this way. I imagine that in eating and drinking we are lifted up into the presence of Christ by the power of the Holy Spirit. The Spirit takes us into the throne room of God to feed on Christ, that is, to be nourished by the power of his resurrected life. Through eating the bread and drinking the wine, the Spirit pours life into us by virtue of the life-giving new humanity of Jesus Christ.

Jesus is *on the table* through the bread and wine. But it is not the dead body of Christ; it is a living, resurrected new creation.

Conclusion

The horizon of the Christian faith is the eschaton. New creation is the essence of the Christian definition of salvation. Through baptism we are created anew, raised to a new life, seated in the heavenlies, and initiated into the body of Christ. In the Lord's supper we "remember" the new creation as we sit at table with the risen Christ and are nourished by his life.

Through baptism we are raised to sit in the heavenlies with Christ as co-rulers in the new creation. Like the original couple in Genesis, we are called to live as a royal priesthood within God's creation. Living within this old age we are the instruments of the new age as we walk in the power of the Spirit who renews all things.

In the Lord's supper, we "remember the future"[3] because the new human, Jesus the Messiah, is present at the table as an earnest of the future. At the table, we experience the presence of the living Christ both as host and through feeding on his immortal life. In this way the supper is, as the ancient martyr Ignatius called it, the "medicine of immortality" (*Letter to the Ephesians* 20:2). It is an antidote to death, despair, and destruction precisely because the living presence of the risen Lord communes with us, nourishes us, and assures us.

Chapter 6

"ENTER THE WATER"—
Renewed Vision for Practice

To suggest a renewed vision does not mean that everything we have believed about or practiced around baptism should be jettisoned. Quite the contrary, renewal involves remembering, rekindling, and revitalizing the truths and habits that embody its essence. It means immersing ourselves in the story of Scripture, its theological vision, and discerning ways to practice that vision in the contemporary church.

Below I begin with a theological vision that I hope will renew its practice in our communities. The driving question is: How might we practice the kingdom of God in ways that embody the theology embedded in the story of God?

A Theological Vision for the Water

In 1982 the Faith and Order Commission of the World Council of Churches adopted the text of a significant ecumenical statement entitled *Baptism, Eucharist and Ministry* (known as *BEM*).[1] Widely distributed, it is the most frequently studied document produced by the ecumenical movement. It has become a significant starting point for discussion between different faith communities, and many have adopted it. *BEM* has become a consensus document of sorts.

BEM organizes the "meaning of baptism" around five theological ideas. As the product of a thorough discussion of Scripture and the interaction of multiple Christian communions, the simplicity and depth of these points are captivating.

1. Baptism as Participation in Christ's Death and Resurrection
2. Baptism as Conversion, Pardoning, and Cleansing
3. Baptism as the Gift of the Spirit
4. Baptism as Incorporation into the Body of Christ
5. Baptism as the Sign of the Kingdom

These helpful points summarize the theology of baptism in a profound way.

Five Themes

I explored these themes in earlier chapters if not exactly in the same language. *BEM*'s own explanatory summaries are worth reading; I recommend them to you. However, I will summarize these themes in my own words so that (1) I might draw on this theology in the rest of the chapter, and (2) I might recap the theological meaning of baptism drawn from the story of God in previous chapters.

Participation in Christ's Death and Resurrection. Though the heading only includes "death and resurrection," the BEM explanation adds "life" to the "death and resurrection of Jesus Christ." This is important. The baptism of Jesus is the starting point for thinking about Christian baptism. Our exodus through the water with Jesus is the beginning of a partnership with Jesus in ministry. We follow Jesus into the water in order to follow him in his ministry. We pass through the waters so that we might know freedom—not only the freedom from bondage but a freedom that enables us to live and participate in the ministry of Jesus.

Our baptism also participates in the death and resurrection of Jesus. We die with Jesus in baptism as our old person is crucified and a new one is raised to life. We transition from life to death. Jesus' death becomes our death and his resurrected life becomes our life. Dying with Christ, we die to sin and are thus freed from sin. Raised with Christ, we live again and are thus called to a life of holiness and righteousness. This life, however, is not only about our present sanctification; it is the promise of a resurrection life that destroys death itself. We are freed not only from the guilt and power of sin but from the throes of death itself. This is new creation, which we presently experience in new life but also in the promise of resurrection when God will transform the cosmos, including our bodies. Baptism, then, is our union with Christ in our present sanctification and in our future resurrection. Our baptism means we participate in new humanity, which is Christ.

Conversion, Pardoning, and Cleansing. Just as Jesus affirmed solidarity with sinners by submitting to a baptism of repentance for the forgiveness of sins, so we confess our sins in submitting to the same. The baptismal waters are our conversion or turning; they are a moment of repentance. Our baptism announces that we have turned away from sin and affirmed our allegiance to the kingdom of God. Through baptism we commit ourselves to following Jesus; we embrace discipleship. This baptism, moreover, is more than human commitment; it is also a divine cleansing. We are washed, cleansed, and pardoned. Baptism is linked to the forgiveness of sins, justification, and sanctification. Our conversion narrative is incomplete without baptism.

The Gift of the Spirit. While the Spirit is active in the lives of people in many ways and diverse times, the gift of the Spirit is promised to the baptized. Baptism and this gift are so linked that one is incomplete without the other. This redemptive presence, which is the glory of God dwelling within us, is poured out on the baptized as a seal that they belong to God and are heirs of the glory to come. This presence transforms and empowers us, and this gift assures our future in Christ. Baptism is an eschatological event where the Spirit anoints us just as Jesus was anointed at his baptism. Through the presence of the Spirit we cry "Abba."

Incorporation into the Body of Christ. Baptism into Christ is baptism into the body of Christ. We all share a common baptism since there is only one baptism in which God unites us with Christ and anoints us with the Spirit. In the one Spirit we are baptized into the one body. This union transcends all other allegiances; indeed, it reduces all other allegiances to nothing. There is no national, ethnic, gender, or social distinctions within the body; our baptism means we are one though diversely gifted. This one baptism embodies our shared communion in one God, one Lord, and one Spirit. United in one communion, together we confess, serve, and praise the Triune God.

Sign of the Kingdom. Just as John prepared a people for the kingdom of God through a baptismal cleansing, so God translates us into the kingdom through a baptismal cleansing. It is a moment of transition from the kingdom of Satan into the kingdom of God. Thus, through baptism, we are already members of the kingdom that has not yet fully come. Our baptism bears witness to the reality of the new creation in which we already participate but also embodies the hope of our full participation through resurrection and the redemption of the cosmos. Our baptism marks us as kingdom people whose allegiance is to the kingdom of God; we serve no other kingdom. Our baptism marks us as people who belong to the future and are committed to, by the power of the Spirit and in the unity of God's people, realizing that future in the present.

The Meaning of Baptism: A Theological Convergence?

My heritage is the Churches of Christ, which is part of the Stone-Campbell Movement. I love my heritage and I believe it has much to contribute to contemporary Christianity. This is particularly true of its sacramental theology. At one time there was a close, though uneasy, association between the forefathers of Churches of Christ and Southern Baptists, but this ultimately resulted in a clear division between the two communions.

In the light of recent developments in both communities, a potential reproachment is emerging between some. A convergence is possible within the paradigm shift currently in play.[2] In my opinion, four points are shaping this converging baptismal theology, and these four points are only a beginning point for future dialogue.

First, baptism is part of the conversion narrative of the early church. It is neither an appendage to conversion nor merely the first act of congregational membership. It is part of the process of becoming a Christian in the biblical text. While this is standard teaching among Churches of Christ, it is increasingly recognized among Baptists. Robert Stein's 1998 article, "Baptism and Becoming a Christian in the New Testament," initiated this discussion among Southern Baptists.[3] In dialogue with Stone-Campbell scholars, Wayne House "enthusiastically acknowledge[d], contrary to the common practice in Baptist churches, that the early church would not have understood a person claiming to be a Christian who was not baptized."[4] Broadman & Holman's 2006 publication entitled *Believer's Baptism* affirms this thesis in several places. Stein, for example, concludes his essay with the statement that "water-baptism 'in/into the name of Jesus/Lord Jesus/Jesus Christ' is understood as an essential part of becoming a Christian."[5] Both Stein and Thomas Schreiner consistently refer to the biblical use of "synecdoche" where "faith," "repentance," and "baptism" can stand for the whole conversion process.[6] A. B. Caneday boldly states: "Baptism is an indispensable aspect of conversion along with at least four other elements: repentance, faith, confession, and regeneration."[7] Baptism, he concludes, is part of the "normal conversion pattern."[8]

Second, baptism, as a means of grace, has soteriological meaning. While Churches of Christ have not generally used the sacramental language of "means of grace," they typically teach that baptism is the appointed act through which believers are forgiven of their sins. British Baptists and the Baptist World Alliance have affirmed this kind of sacramentalism in their baptismal theology. Some U.S. Baptists use this language. James McClendon described baptism as an "effectual sign" which is a divine "yes" to humanity's cry for salvation; baptism is "an act of God."[9] Even more conservative Baptists, such as Wayne Grudem, describe baptism as a "means of grace" and reject those who argue that baptism is *"merely symbolic"* and "that the Holy Spirit *does not* work through it."[10] Another example from the recent Broadman & Holman publication is Caneday who heads his article's conclusion with the title "Baptism as Means of Grace" and endorses Alexander Campbell's distinction between baptism as an instrumental cause rather than an efficient cause.[11] Baptism is a performative sign through which God has chosen to mediate his grace as believers entrust themselves to Christ by the power of the Spirit.

Third, baptism serves faith and is subordinate to its soteriological function. A major premise in John Calvin's sacramental theology is that the sacraments serve faith (*Institutes of Christian Religion*, 4.14.13). Though baptism was ordinarily the means by which God acted to save, according to Calvin, baptism is not absolutely necessary to salvation. Indeed, faith is more important than baptism, and baptism is an "inferior mean" [*sic*] though it is a confirmation of forgiveness through faith.[12] He rejects the idea that only the baptized might be saved and thus rejects that rationale for emergency baptisms (*Institutes*, 4.15.20). In other words, baptism is God's ordinary means of grace but not an absolute one. Faith is the more fundamental means. This is evidenced in the Gospels themselves as Jesus forgives sin through faith without baptism (cf. Luke 5:20; 7:48-50). Further, in Paul salvation is from "faith to faith," which roots the means of salvation in faith (Rom. 1:17). Even though baptism may participate in the instrumentality of faith as a means, faith is still the more fundamental principle.

While this perspective is not commonly heard among members of the Churches of Christ, it was Alexander Campbell's. He compares one who is unimmersed to an imperfect Christian. He cannot bring himself to deny that any person who "is acting up to the full measure of his knowledge," and has not been "negligent, according to his opportunities, to ascertain the will of his Master" is a Christian. He feels that if he were to paganize all the unimmersed, he would be "a pure sectarian, a Pharisee among Christians." Therefore, he cannot regard the pious unimmersed as "aliens from Christ and the well-grounded hope of heaven."[13] The God who has "always enjoined upon man 'mercy, rather than sacrifice'" has "never demanded" baptism "as [an] indispensable condition of salvation."[14] Campbell never made immersion a *sine qua non* of eternal salvation. Indeed, Campbell felt that some had "given to baptism an undue eminence—a sort of pardon-procuring, rather than a pardon-certifying and enjoying efficacy."[15] Unfortunately, such fears were fully realized among some within Churches of Christ.

Fourth, salvation is a process of transformation into the image of Christ that gives baptism its theological significance and limits its soteriological importance. Whereas some within Churches of Christ saw "transformed" unimmersed people as rebellious, Campbell did not think their non-immersion a hindrance to recognizing their "inward" baptism. "Sir," he asks, "will not his uncircumcision, or unbaptism, be counted to him for baptism?"[16] The transformation of character is more important than a single misunderstood command of God. Campbell refused to "make any one duty the standard of Christian state or character, not even immersion into the name of the Father, of the Son, and of the Holy Spirit." He would not make baptism the single or most significant identifying marker of Christianity—he would "not substitute obedience to one commandment, for universal or even for general obedience."[17] Transformation, then, was more important than baptism and this is precisely because baptism served the goal of transformation and was not itself the goal. Campbell led believers down in the river to experience the assurance of God's gracious forgiveness as part of God's transforming work, but some of his theological descendants went down in the river to draw a line in the sand. They turned baptism into a legal technicality rather than a divine work of transforming assurance.

Churches of Christ and Southern Baptists can move closer to each other if, on the one hand, those within Churches of Christ adopt a baptismal theology that recognizes the primacy of faith and the goal of transformation and, on the other hand, Baptists adopt a baptismal theology that recognizes baptism as a means of grace within the ordinary conversion narrative. Pragmatically, Churches of Christ could cease questioning or doubting the eternal destiny of unimmersed believers and recognize them as pilgrims in the process of transformation on the same journey as themselves, and Baptists could invite believers to baptism as part of their conversion experience and invite seekers to baptism as the sinner's prayer itself. That is what I would call a biblical convergence.

Baptismal Practices

Baptism is a controversial topic. Believers have disagreed about the mode, subject, and design of baptism as well as the best way to practice baptism within the church's liturgy. While impossible to cover that range of questions in the brief space allotted here, several questions are particularly pressing within communities that only baptize believers, particularly Churches of Christ.

Children, Church, and Believer's Baptism

What is the relationship of our children to the kingdom of God?

Advocates of believer's baptism, at least within the Stone-Campbell Movement, have historically held that children are "safe" (without sin) until they reach the "age of accountability" at which time they own their sin and become sinners (guilty).

At that point, they are outside the grace of God. They do not belong to the kingdom. Consequently, children are instructed about their sin, faith in Jesus, and baptism. As a result, baptistic churches usually reap a baptismal harvest among their children between the ages of eight and twelve. (I myself was baptized by my father when I was eleven.)

This approach assumes that children move from "safe" to "lost" and then are "saved" when they are baptized. (I was baptized so that I would not go to hell!) The tricky point, however, is how to identify the exact time and circumstance when they move from "safe" to "lost." Existentially, this is an important question. If a child dies at the age of ten unbaptized, is the child "safe" or "lost"? What if the child is thirteen or fifteen? It is a harsh but living question.

I would hope that we might all have the grace to say the deceased child now experiences the embrace of the loving Father covered in the mercy of Jesus. But on what theological or biblical grounds do we say that if we believe that children within the church move from "safe" to "lost" at some point which we cannot certainly identify?

When I baptized my daughter at the age of eleven, I know with absolute certainty that if she had died the night before I would have "preached her into heaven" (as the saying goes). In my mind, at least, my daughter was not baptized to move her from "lost" to "saved."

So what do we do with this theological impasse? I suppose one could argue that my love for my daughter blinded me to her "lostness." I suppose one could suggest that she was not ready for baptism if she was not "lost" and perhaps she was baptized too early. But I question the theological under-pinnings of the notion that our children move from "safe" to "lost" to "saved" (once baptized).

My daughter always believed in Jesus. There was never a time when she did not believe. Her faith developed through various levels of understanding and discipleship but her faith was always there. From her first singings of "Jesus Loves Me" to her confession of faith at her baptism, faith was a constant in her life.

What do I do with that? I believe that through faith she was not merely "safe" but "saved," that is, living in communion and relationship with God as her faith developed and her discipleship matured. As our children grow up in faith and live within a faith community, they enjoy relationship with God through family, community, and their own faith.

Their growth in faith is marked throughout their family and communal life. Some faith communities have rituals to mark the various moments of faith, even something as simple as reciting the Lord's Prayer or as dramatic as a "graduation into the Youth Group." The most dramatic, biblical, and ini-tiatory ritual is baptism.

When our children who have been nurtured in faith and have expressed their faith in a multitude of ways come to bap-tism, I do not believe they come as "lost" people. Rather, they come as children of the church, children of the faith commu-nity. They come already belonging to the kingdom of God—they are neither "lost" nor "safe" but already in communion with God.

They come to baptism to declare their faith. They come to publicly embrace their discipleship. They come to become full participants in the life of the faith community through owning their own faith and committing themselves to following Jesus to the cross. They follow Jesus into the water in order to follow him to the cross.

Baptism for our children is a climatic act of faith. It dramatically initiates them into a life of discipleship which they have now owned as full participants within the community.

The baptism of Jesus is a model for this. Jesus did not come to his baptism as one who was "lost." He came to his baptism to declare his discipleship—a follower of the Father who intended to do the will of the Father, even to cross. His baptism began his public ministry, his public life, as a disciple. But he had been a disciple long before his baptism. He had been nurtured in faith by Joseph and Mary, he had been taught at the synagogue, and he had celebrated Israel's redemption at the Passover. In effect, he had matured as a disciple through his first thirty years and owned his mission at his baptism in obedience to the Father.

Our children do something analogous. They have been nurtured by family and community. They have walked a path of faith and discipleship throughout their years. And when they come to their baptism, they do not come as "lost" little people. They come as believers—people who have lived in relationship with God since their birth—ready to own their discipleship, declare their allegiance to the Father, and commit to the way of the cross as followers of Jesus.

This view of baptism is a bit higher than just moving from "lost" to "saved." To convince children they have done bad things and that they need forgiveness is a much simpler task than to wait for them to own their discipleship and commit to the way of the cross.

Perhaps if we thought that our children lived in communion with God through faith we would not rush them to the water as soon as they become aware of some distinctions about good and evil. Perhaps if we thought our children were saved by God's grace through faith, we could patiently wait for the moment when they are fourteen or sixteen or even eighteen for them to declare their discipleship and take up the mission of Jesus.

I am not suggesting a particular age for baptism. I do not know what that is. Everyone must decide for themselves. What I am suggesting is that to pressure our children into baptism in order to soothe our own fears about their salvation is misguided and dangerous.

Rebaptism?

This question has at least two dimensions. Some seek rebaptism because they feel that their first immersion as a believer was defective. Others feel their infant baptism was authentic and see no need to express their faith through "another" baptism.

Some adults are reimmersed because they believe their baptism as a pre-teen was for less than laudable motives. Some associate their baptism with a kind of "following the crowd" syndrome, or some believe their baptism was purely an emotive response to the passionate appeal of a persuasive evangelist. Other adults are reimmersed because they believe they lacked a sufficient understanding of the meaning of baptism. For example, they may come to believe that one must understand that baptism is the moment of salvation in order for God to work effectively through it. Consequently, they are reimmersed.

Both miss the point. The efficacy of baptism does not depend upon what we believe about baptism but whether we trust in Christ. The object of faith is Christ, not baptism. The efficacy of baptism is the efficacy of faith, and faith is effective when it trusts in Christ's work for us (Col. 2:12). The important question, then, is whether we trusted in Christ for our salvation when we were immersed. We should not focus on the perfection of faith since that is unattainable. Rather, we focus on the object of faith—in whom do we trust? When we remember our faith in Christ at our baptism, then our baptism is a divine promise to us.

We all were baptized with mixed motives and misunderstandings. While we may have been persuaded by an evangelist or peers or moved by the emotional drama of the occasion (including the fear of going to hell if we were not baptized that very night!), the significant point is that when we were immersed we trusted in Christ. If that trust was present at our baptism, whether other motives were there or not, then God was graciously present through that faith. God's promise in baptism is attached to faith and where faith is present God is present. Generally speaking, if one has enough faith in Christ to be baptized in submission to God's command, then God will graciously receive that faith no matter what other misunderstandings or inferior motives are present. Enough faith to act is sufficient faith.

If faith, however, is so central as a means for baptismal efficacy, what does this say about infant baptism? Should those baptized as infants be immersed as believers and thus be "rebaptized"?

I appreciate how significant infant baptism is for believers who were initiated into the Christian faith by their parents. I value parents and grandparents who seek to introduce and nurture their children in faith. I would not want to devalue the nurture and training that those so raised have received. Further, I would not want anyone to repudiate the values that their baptism represents and which their parents sought to instill in them.

I do believe, however, that infant baptism is incomplete and does not reflect a biblical baptismal theology. I call those baptized as infants to express their own personal faith and discipleship through immersion. By so doing, I do not ask anyone to renounce everything that was part of their past. Indeed, they affirm their past by a continued, though fuller, commitment to Christ.

McClendon refers to the immersion of a believer who was first baptized as an infant as a baptismal "repair." Rebaptism is not a denial of one's life of faith up to that moment, but a reaffirmation of faith. The "appropriate remedy for an impaired baptism," McClendon writes, is repetition whereby "this repetitive act *regularize[s] the original one* rather than" denying "its [impaired] existence" so that "baptismal repair" acknowledges "the earlier rite and the genuine faith that has appeared."[18]

I affirm the rebaptism of those baptized as infants for the same reason I reject the rebaptism of those who were baptized as believers. Baptism is effective through faith, just as grace is received through faith. Every immersion that expresses faith in Christ is effective by the grace of God, but no baptism without faith is complete.

Baptismal Liturgy

While many traditions have elaborate and well-developed baptismal liturgies or services, my own experience with my heritage is that baptisms are independent events. They often stand alone. They are often private moments in a gathering of intimate friends and family. Even when they are part of the assembly, as responses to the sermon's invitation, they function as addendums to the church's worship. Frequently, baptisms are brief, even hasty, moments disconnected from the liturgy, worship, and life of the church. This is unfortunate, and it diminishes the significance of the baptismal event.

It is rather surprising that some within Churches of Christ, who have such a high view of baptism, functionally reduce baptism to a private, brief, and isolated act of obedience. The roots of this inclination are too complicated to explore here, though the individualistic heritage of Churches of Christ and the contemporary privatization of faith contribute to the process.

One response to this trend is to give more focused attention to baptismal liturgy. In other words, wrap baptism in the clothing of Word, worship, and community, and connect baptism with the grand story of the Christian faith. I was reminded of this need when I heard how my good friends Dean and Melanie Barham approached the baptism of their daughter, Christine. Her baptismal liturgy intersected her faith story, God's story, and the community of faith with her own baptism. In the light of their example, as well as my own experience and review of liturgies, I suggest six components for a baptismal liturgy. These suggestions are not themselves a liturgy nor are they prescriptive. Rather, they suggest a way to frame and enhance the significance of this moment in the life of the believer and the church.

Tell the Story. I am a firm believer that the Word must always be joined with the sacrament, that is, the gospel story grounds, shapes, and gives meaning to baptism. Throughout Acts one reads that people "heard, believed, and were baptized." It is important to hear the story again at our baptism. Jesus is the Messiah, the faithful remnant of Israel. The faithful obedience of God's Messiah redeemed us from sin and death.

The meaning of baptism, grounded in that story, can be told from several vistas—the exodus, the baptism of Jesus, or the death and resurrection of Jesus. Whatever the specific emphasis, baptism is a movement from the brokenness of this old creation to participation in God's new creation. It is liberation from bondage, the descent of the Spirit, and new life.

Rehearse Our Story. I like to hear more from the believer than a few words of confession. I suggest a model something like what happens in Psalm 66 or other thanksgiving Psalms within Israel. Psalm 66 invites the community to first "come and see" as they remember together the story of how God delivered Israel from Egyptian bondage, refined them in the wilderness, and led them into a land of abundance. Then the Psalmist invites the community to "come and listen" as the Psalmist tells the story of his/her own personal deliverance and invites them to join his/her thanksgiving. In the same way the first step in a baptismal liturgy is to proclaim the gospel, and the second step is for believers to rehearse their own faith journey.

Everyone who walks to the edge of the water has a faith story. When we tell our stories the community of faith is encouraged, but they also share the storyteller's thanksgiving to God. Their story may be like the prodigal son's, or it may be something like Saul's experience on the road to Damascus. Or their story may focus on the nurture of their parents or the influence of a mentor. Whatever our journeys to faith may look like, believers should bear witness, offer thanks, and declare their commitment.

Confess the Story. Often the confession at baptism is a simple sentence or even merely a "Yes." I certainly don't want to undervalue the significance of that confession; my next point emphasizes it. At the same time I think it is helpful to confess more than a single sentence. Taking my cue from the earliest baptismal practices of the ancient church, I suggest a more elaborate confession is appropriate. The Apostle's Creed—creed comes form the Latin *credo*, meaning "I believe"—arose out the church's practice of baptismal confession ("the Rule of Faith").

Believers confess:

> I believe in God the Father, almighty, maker of
> heaven and earth.

Then they confess:

> I believe in Jesus Christ, his only begotten Son,
> our Lord,
> who was conceived by the Holy Spirit,
> and born of the virgin Mary.
> He suffered under Pontius Pilate,
> was crucified, died, and was buried,
> he descended into Hades.
> The third day he rose again from the dead.
> He ascended to heaven
> and is seated at the right hand of God the
> Father almighty

Then they confess:

> I believe in the Holy Spirit,
> the holy universal church,
> the communion of the saints,
> the forgiveness of sins,
> the resurrection of the body,
> and life everlasting.

This confession not only affirms the story (including a Triune confession), but also rehearses it in a way that unites the believer with what the church has confessed throughout the centuries.

This historic confession moves from creation to new creation through the work of the Triune God who creates, redeems, and communes. It confesses the narrative of creation, incarnation, and recreation. It acknowledges the centrality of the work of the Messiah whose death, resurrection, and ascension inaugurates new creation. It affirms the present reality of new creation through the forgiveness of sins and the communion of the saints while at the same time hopefully anticipating the resurrection of the body and everlasting life in the new heaven and new earth.

The confession may function something like a wedding vow both in practice and meaning. In practice, the confessor might repeat the words after the administrator speaks them. This is how the Barhams used it in Christine's baptism. Acknowledging the work of the Triune God, Christine responded to Father's act in Jesus through the Spirit by confessing the story and, through faith, vowing her commitment to live within that story. It is not that we simply assent to the truth of the story, but that we also enter the story and own it as ours. Baptism responds to God's work for us and pledges our allegiance to the story God has enacted.

Confess the Messiah. In one sense to include the "good confession," that is, "I believe that Jesus is the Messiah, the Son of the living God," is redundant. This is confessed when we confess the story. But I think it is still a poignant moment to embrace because it is central to the Gospel narratives themselves. In Matthew 16, Mark 8, and Luke 9, Peter's confession at Caesarea Philippi is the turning point in their Gospels. Prior to that time, Jesus is engaged in the ministry of the kingdom of God as he proclaims the good news of the kingdom and practices the kingdom through healings, exorcisms, and reconciling tables. When, however, Peter confesses Jesus as the Messiah, the attention of the Gospels (especially Mark) turns to the passion narrative. The confession announces the cross and resurrection.

When we make the "good confession," we, too, are announcing our intent to follow Jesus by dying to self. This confession is no mere assent but a commitment to follow Jesus to the cross. This is the confession of a disciple, an apprentice to the life of Jesus. When we make the "good confession," we commit ourselves to the path of discipleship.

Enact the Story. Surrounding the actual baptism itself with numerous symbols is helpful and meaningful. For example, we may wear white baptismal robes, we may have a change of clothing ready after the baptism to symbolize "putting on Christ" in baptism, or we may raise our hands as we announce that this baptism is "in the name of the Father, Son, and Spirit." The church throughout history has used many different symbols to communicate the meaning of this moment. I would not discourage any helpful symbol.

At the core, however, is the enactment of the story. In this moment the sacrament performs the story; it re-enacts it. In one sense, we follow Jesus into the water. Jesus went into the water praying, which is an appropriate model for us as well. Our baptism is a prayer, and bathing it in prayer accentuates this point. Coming out of the water, Jesus hears the words, "You are my beloved child; I am delighted with you." I think it is important to speak those words over those who arise from the water. Those words belong to them since they have followed Jesus into the water. In this moment we might also acknowledge the descent of the Spirit, even symbolizing it through an anointing or a laying on of hands. Just as Jesus was anointed with the Spirit, so the baptized are anointed as well. Like Jesus, the baptized are empowered to encounter temptation and practice the ministry of the kingdom as God's beloved children.

In another sense, our baptism participates in the death and resurrection of Jesus. This is a movement from sin to forgiveness, from slavery to freedom, from death to life. Through baptism we are buried with Christ, raised with Christ, and seated with Christ in the heavenlies. It is important, I think, to acknowledge this movement. In some traditions, baptisms are often focused on the forgiveness of sins. In other traditions, they stress the public testimony of faith. I think it goes deeper than either. Rather, it initiates us—"baptized into Christ"—into new life, new creation. This is the experience of new creation itself, which entails participation in the communion of the Triune God ("baptizing them into the name of the Father, Son and Spirit"), the communion of the saints ("baptized into the body of Christ"), and resurrection life itself ("raised to walk in newness of life"). Baptism embodies new creation; it is a divine act of recreation.

Celebrate in Community. Since baptism is a new exodus out of old creation (enslavement) into new creation (liberation), the model of Exodus 14-15 is enlightening. The communal celebration of Exodus 15:1-2 should galvanize our own celebrations of baptism.

I will sing to the Lord
for he has triumphed gloriously…
The Lord is my strength and my might,
and he has become my salvation;
this is my God, and I will praise him,
my father's God, and I will exalt him.

This praise was communal. Through baptism we are plunged into a community that stretches across time from Israel into the future. We crossed the sea with Israel, and now we rejoice with Israel. More than that, we join the heavenly chorus of praise among those who already stand by the sea with the Lamb, singing the "song of Moses, the servant of God, and the song of the Lamb" (Rev. 15:3-4).

Great and amazing are your deeds,
Lord God the Almighty!
Just and true are your ways,
King of the nations!
Lord, who will not fear
and glorify your name?
For you alone are holy.
All nations will come and worship before you,
for your judgments have been revealed.

Praise and song should surround our exodus moments, our baptisms, and this includes community. The exodus is a heavenly liturgy played out on earth. The heavenly host rejoices and God delights in the moment because we have been baptized in the sea (water) and cloud (Spirit) with Israel. We have been washed in the Spirit (1 Cor. 6:11).

I realize that baptism has become, for some, a private event. While this is sometimes appropriate—as when one wants to be baptized the "same hour of the night"—the communal meaning of baptism and its invitation for communal celebration locate baptism more solidly in the community itself. I don't mean that baptism is only appropriate in response to the sermon's invitation. I mean much more. Rather, I would hope that baptisms themselves would be integrated into the assembly itself and become part of the liturgical life of the church as it gathers weekly. Even when a baptism was at "the same hour of the night," the community can join in the celebration if there is a video or some kind of significant liturgical moment to embrace the baptized. If their baptism was private, let the congregation encircle them, hug them, and accept them by some kind of communal ritual that highlights that they have been "baptized into one body."

Conclusion

What does baptism mean to you? What single word or phrase would best describe your experience? Whatever our "word," it arises from both our theology and our practice. Without theology, our practice is meaningless. Without practices that embody that theology, we experience dissonance. In either case baptism becomes irrelevant, unnecessary, or merely symbolic.

Renewed practice needs a renewed theological vision, and renewed theology needs practice in order to fully experience what God gives. Baptism is the story of God put into practice, and through that practice God gives Christ to us in a concrete way. Baptism is the gospel in water. God unites us with Christ, liberates us from slavery to death in the old creation, raises us with Christ to live a new life, and seats us with Christ in the heavenlies to reign with him. In baptism we follow Jesus into the water that we might embrace the mission for which God created humanity. We follow Jesus from the water into the wilderness to the cross in the hope of inheriting a new world. That is the baptism of Jesus, and it is also our baptism.

Chapter 7

"COME TO THE TABLE"—
Renewed Vision for Practice

To suggest a renewed vision does not mean that everything we have believed about or practiced around the table should be jettisoned. Quite the contrary, renewal involves remembering, rekindling, and revitalizing the truths and habits that embody the essence of the table. It means immersing ourselves in the story of Scripture, its theological vision, and discerning ways to practice that vision in contemporary church.

Below I begin with a theological vision that I hope will drive a renewed practice of the table in our communities. The driving question is: How might we practice the kingdom of God at the table in ways that embody the theology embedded in the story of God?

A Theological Vision for the Table

In 1982 the Faith and Order Commission of the World Council of Churches adopted a significant ecumenical statement entitled *Baptism, Eucharist and Ministry* (known as *BEM*).[1] Widely distributed, it is the most widely studied document produced by the modern ecumenical movement. It has become a significant starting-point for discussion between different faith communities, and many have adopted it. In some sense, *BEM* has become a consensus document though there are still many points of divergence.

BEM organizes the "meaning of the Eucharist" around five theological ideas. As the product of a thorough discussion of Scripture and the interaction of multiple Christian communions, the simplicity and the depth of each of these points are captivating.

1. The Eucharist as Thanksgiving to the Father
2. The Eucharist as Anamnesis or Memorial of Christ
3. The Eucharist as Invocation of the Spirit
4. The Eucharist as Communion of the Faithful
5. The Eucharist as Meal of the Kingdom

These helpful points summarize the theology of the Lord's Supper in a profound way.

Five Themes

I explored these themes in earlier chapters if not exactly in the same language. *BEM*'s own explanatory summaries are worth reading. However, I will summarize these themes in my own words so that (1) I might draw on this theology in the rest of the chapter, and (2) I might recap the theological meaning of the supper drawn from the story of God in previous chapters.

Thanksgiving to the Father. Jesus himself gave thanks to the Father at the table with his disciples. The Father supplies both the bread through creation *and* the body of Christ. We give thanks for bread as we recognize the gift of God's good creation as well as how God became flesh for our salvation. As a meal, we are grateful for the nourishment God provides through the creation. But there is more. When we eat and drink we give thanks for the Father's gift of the Son as we celebrate the work of God in Christ since the bread is also the body of Christ. The Lord's supper is, by the example of Jesus, a thanksgiving (a eucharist).

Memorial of Christ. Jesus told his disciples to remember him. He did not ask them to remember his death, but to remember *him.* We remember what God has done for us in Christ and how Christ as acted on our behalf. We remember the incarnation, ministry, death, resurrection, and ascension of Jesus the Messiah—the whole "event" which is the meaning of Christ's work from incarnation to the second coming. We remember the gospel. This memory, however, is no mere cognitive reflection on a past event. Rather, it is the present experience of the Christ Event. "To remember" is to experience the present reality of God in Christ reconciling the world to God's self. We "remember" our redemption just as Israel "remembered" its own every year in the Passover, that is, we see ourselves as members of the redeemed community. To "remember" is to share in the story of God as part of the people of God.

Invocation of the Spirit. Christ is present at the table and given to us through the bread and fruit of the vine by the work of the Holy Spirit. The Spirit is the one through whom we commune with the Father through the risen Christ. Just as Jesus was raised in the power of the Spirit, so we are raised to the heavenlies to feed on Christ, experience his living presence, and commune with the Father through the Son (Eph. 2:18). The Spirit brings us to the Son and unites us with him in authentic communion, and by this we experience the "communion of the Spirit" in a concrete, sacramental way (2 Cor. 13:13). The eschatological Spirit transforms the old creation signs of bread and wine into the new creation experiences of the body and blood of Christ through which the living Christ nourishes us.

Communion of the Faithful. This meal nourishes the church and unites it through eating from one loaf and drinking from one cup, that is, Christ himself. We are one new body through the body of Christ, and we are one new people through the blood of Christ. When we commune in the body and blood of Christ through eating and drinking we bear witness to that unity and experience its spiritual and visible reality. This communion of believers, however, is not limited by space and time. Since this communion takes place in the heavenlies we are united with the church throughout the world and the people of God throughout time. We eat and drink as the one people of God despite our diverse geographic, ethnic, and temporal realities. In this sense the table is an intensely communal event. We not only commune with the Father, Son, and Spirit, but we commune with each other as the Spirit unites the whole church—past, present, and future—in this one moment of eating and drinking.

The Meal of the Kingdom. The future is already present at the table of the Lord as we sit at the Messianic banquet with all the people of God. The table in the church is the table of the kingdom of God that celebrates the reconciliation of all peoples, ethnicities, and nations as well as the redemption of creation itself. The Lord's supper is a foretaste, a present experience, of the future. We participate in new creation through it. The supper, then, calls us into the mission of God for the reconciliation of the world and the renewal of creation, and the supper—which by God's grace nourishes us with the power of new creation—transforms us into the image of Christ and empowers us for mission for the sake of the world. We receive Christ to become Christ to the world.

Four Practicalities

The above summary highlights four significant points.

First, the table is no mere memorial. On the contrary, it is a divine act. God does something through our eating and drinking. Christ is present to commune with us, nourish us, empower us, and comfort us so that we might follow him and fully invest ourselves in the mission of God.

Too often we reduce the supper to mere symbolism by either theology or practice or both. This leads to a focus on human action as if the meaning of the supper is wholly dependent upon us (how we remember, what we think about, how introspective we are, whether we do it right, etc.). This turns the supper into our meal rather than the supper of the Lord, and we turn the supper into some kind of human-centered activity rather than gratefully receiving God's gifts.

When we eat and drink, we are not the only actors. God is doing something as well. God is giving Christ to us through the bread and wine. In this moment, God assures us that Christ is for us. In this moment, God loves us in Christ. As surely as we taste the bread and drink the cup, so we are assured that we are beloved by God and united with Christ through the Spirit by faith.

Second, the Lord's table is a communal event. It is not an individualistic act. We don't sit alone. On the contrary, we sit with the whole church, not only the ones gathered in the same assembly but also the universal church gathered in the heavenlies. We are many members but we eat as one body; we commune with each other as well as with the Triune God.

Unfortunately many tend to think about the supper as their private moment with God. It is as if they wait the whole week—filled with its busyness—for these few minutes to privately commune with God in silence. This subverts the communal intent of the supper. Private moments with God are important, necessary, and wonderful, but the Lord's supper is not one of them. This is a communal moment with God.

The table of the Lord is for communion with both God and the people of God. It functions both vertically and horizontally. God meets us at the table as a people, not as isolated individuals. Community can neither be assumed nor ignored when we eat together; the table must embody community in practical ways.

Third, the Lord's table is an experience of the future. As the kingdom meal, we eat and drink at the Messianic banquet whenever we sit at the Lord's table. New creation, the future of creation as new heaven and new earth, has already arrived in the resurrection of Jesus, and at the table we eat with the living Christ. With the eyes of faith we see our future in the one who sits at the table as the living host. When we eat and drink we experience, participate in, and bear witness to the future kingdom of God as new creation when God transforms the creation, including our own bodies. The table is a proleptic experience of hope, joy, and comfort.

Fourth, the Lord's table is an experience of grace and assurance. As we eat and drink in faith, we receive the bread and wine as God's assurance that Christ is given to us. As Jesus said, the body is given "for you" and the blood is poured out "for you." The Lord's supper is a concrete moment by which we know that we belong to Christ, to each other, and that, as the song "Blessed Assurance" rings out, "Christ is mine!" We do not approach the table of the Lord in fear and guilt, but in faith that is assured through eating and drinking. The table offers mercy and grace rather than judgment and condemnation for those who trust in Christ.

These perspectives change the mood of the table from visions of past sorrow, gore, and horror into visions of grace, resurrection, new creation, and unending thanksgivings. I often hear comments from my students about the depressing mood of the Lord's supper in the congregations they attend. Though we understand that the death of Jesus was a regrettable necessity, we boast and rejoice in the sacrifice of Christ because it is our redemption; the gospel is good news! At the same time, the table is not simply about a past memory but a present grace and a realized hope.

While we might stress any number of ways in which Christ is present at the table, his presence as host is particularly significant for revisioning the practice of the table. If we believe that Christ is actually present as the living host of the table, then this transforms the table from a solemn, sad, even funerary occasion to a festive celebration. We eat with joy because we eat with the living Christ.

Table-Practice in Community

Our practice of the Lord's supper is layered with centuries of tradition. Some of these traditions effectively embody the supper's meaning while others seem like distant relics. Some traditions hinder while others enrich. This section would be much too long (and probably too boring) if I attempted to identify which traditions help and which hurt. Instead, I will take another approach.

"If I had it *my* way. . . ." This is my wish list for practicing the theological vision described in this chapter. Of course, it would be a fundamental violation of the communal nature of the supper if I demanded "my way," or if I controlled or manipulated the circumstances so that any congregation did exactly what I wanted. I don't have such control nor do I want it. The supper should be a communal experience rather than an expression of my own individual point of view. So my purpose is rhetorical rather than prescriptive.

Below I suggest five practices ("my way") that might help a congregation more fully practice the theological vision of the supper. I don't experience these practices every Sunday myself. Sometimes they are present; sometimes they are not. So what I offer here is a practical vision toward which congregations might move. I would like to see number one practiced, but when it is not at least number two might be. And if number two is not, then at least number three, and so on down the line. In the final analysis, however, in whatever way the church eats the bread and drinks the wine together, my heart can still rejoice in the living Christ who sits at table with us—even in the most "traditional" of services! Christ's presence does not depend on these suggestions.

Practice One: Renew the Meal. Every example of the Lord's supper in the New Testament is a meal, and this is consistent with antecedent Hebrew festivals as well as the anticipated Messianic banquet in the new heaven and new earth. Nothing will invest the table of the Lord with "tableness" more than a meal—a meal in honor of, in memory of (remembering), and in gratitude for Jesus. Meals renew the interactive and horizontal communion of the table—no longer silent and solemn, but joyous and engaging. The supper is not a funerary memorial, but a thanksgiving meal celebrating our salvation through the gospel.

But a meal is difficult with our architecture and problematic for logistical reasons, especially for large congregations. I like the model in Acts 2 where the best of both worlds are present: a general assembly in the temple for teaching/prayer/praise and then a gathering in homes for breaking bread/praise/prayer. I do not, however, advocate the excision of the Lord's supper from the general assembly. Rather, we can observe the supper in both the assembly (more traditionally) and in small groups (as meals). This diversity would actually enrich our experience of the supper.

Practice Two: Renew the Table. Get around a table, even if only for bread and wine. The literal table will produce the atmosphere of table—interaction and face-to-face communion. Gather around standing, or sit at the table. Either way serves a purpose. At least we will not be looking at the backs of each other's heads as we commune with each other. Many traditions ask people to get out of their seats and come to an altar. I prefer asking people to get out of their seats and gather (literally!) around a table where Jesus is the host. At a minimum, it seems to me, a table is important for its symbolism. Even if we remain in our seats to eat and drink, a literal table visible to the assembly embraces the spiritual reality of our faith. The removal of all symbols, particularly any symbol of a table, from some assemblies hinders our spiritual imagination and devalues the importance of symbolism within the assembly.

Practice Three: Renew Community. If we cannot gather around a table where community would occur naturally, we can at least renew the communal dimension in our eating and drinking through corporate prayers, corporate reading of Scripture, congregational singing, encouraging people to prayer with each other, and encouraging each other by verbal interaction. This can be partly accomplished by getting people out of their seats to commune if even merely to stand or turn to people behind them to serve them the communion bread and drink. Invite people to come to the elements instead of bringing the elements to them. As people go to the elements, urge them interact with each other—hugging, greeting, and encouraging each other. The form in which many presently eat the supper screams individualism and discourages active communion between participants.

Practice Four: Renew the Mood. If nothing else, restore the joy of the table to the Lord's supper as a thanksgiving. There is no doubt this is a paradigm shift for western Christians. We have been socialized into a silent, solemn, somber, introspective meditation on the cross of Christ as the focal point of the supper. Unfortunately, this misses the festive nature of our thanksgiving in the presence of the living Christ who hosts the table. It misses the joy of communion itself. We do not commune with a dead Christ but a living one in the power of the Spirit and in gratitude to the Father. Unfortunately, we often eat and drink like it is still Friday rather than Sunday. The mood is set by the kind of prayers we pray, the words that are said at the table, the songs that are sung, and the atmosphere that is set (seating arrangement, lighting, etc.). Changing the mood means investing joy in the moment by recognizing the living Christ is present at the table with us.

Practice Five: Renew the Vision. This is where we must, of course, begin. None of the above is possible without this—a renewed theological vision of the table as communal fellowship with the risen Christ. A new vision is needed, one that will embrace the joy rather than sink into the sorrow of a mere memoralism. I recommend teaching, discussion, communal processing, and more teaching. The vision must change in order to fully experience one through four. But even if one through four are never implemented, a renewed vision and theological understanding will enable people to experience the supper in more significant ways, even if it is only hidden in their own heart. Even in the most somber traditional service, I can still smile as I eat with the living Christ with Joshua at my side.

The presence of Christ does not depend upon an exact form—whether we sit at a table, walk down an aisle, or sit in a pew. It does not depend upon whether we sing before, during, or after. It does not depend on whether there is a meal or simple bread and wine. God effects the presence of Christ in the power of the Spirit through faith as we eat and drink. Form does matter as it may subvert or hinder our experience of what God is doing, but as long as we do not undermine the gospel, Christ is present by God's gracious promise.

The kind of renewal envisioned above, however, is filled with landmines. The traditions surrounding the Lord's supper are deeply entrenched in the piety of a community. This demands extreme sensitivity on the part of those who seek renewal. For many the Lord's supper is symbolic of their own personal piety and a moment of private contemplation on the cross of Christ. This is so ingrained that a shift to thanksgiving and celebration is difficult to imagine and uncomfortable when practiced.

So, how does one move toward the renewal of the Lord's supper in a traditional community? I suggest the following.

+ *Begin slowly*—pray, teach, listen, discuss, and involve the whole community in the process of restudying, rethinking, and revisioning.

+ *Begin small*—make small adjustments in the assembly (for example, using varied Scripture texts for reading at the table), practice this renewal in small groups first, and move toward enjoying the supper in different settings other than in pews (like in a fellowship hall). Make changes in the assembly slowly and only with consensus after periods of discussion and prayer.

+ *Stay inclusive*—remember that there are multiple dimensions embodied in the supper and multiple perspectives legitimately associated with the supper. Consequently, practice the supper in diverse ways to include all these dimensions (including silence), utilize all perspectives and angles for deepening the experience of the supper, and give voice to all persuasions that reflect authentic aspects of the supper.

+ *Stay united*--don't divide the church over something that should unite it. Consequently, be sensitive to years of tradition, recognize how central the piety of this moment is to many and the comfort their past practice gave them, and build a consensus for renewal rather than forcing it or surprising people with change.

+ *Remember the goal*—progress toward the goal of more fully experiencing God and each other at the table. This is the main thing—a communal experience of Jesus' grace and love as we share that love and grace with each other. The main thing is to love God and each other in this moment as well as experience God's love for us.

Table-Practice in House Churches or Small Groups

Often I have been asked how I conduct the Lord's supper as a home meal. Some have wanted to compare their practices with my own, while others have a difficult time imagining how it might be done.

Part of the problem is that most have little idea of what a religious meal looks and feels like. Few Christians have ever experienced an authentic Passover meal or shared a Sabbath meal with Jewish friends. We tend to think of these religious meals as either boringly solemn or riotous parties. But something in between is actually the case.

Religious meals, like the Jewish Passover, are profound but joyous experiences. They are serious rather than frivolous, festive rather than somber. They are moments of memory, fellowship, and praise. They are interactive rather than isolating, communal rather than individualistic. They invite prayer, reflection, and participation. And the Lord's supper is a religious meal—a meal designed to remember Jesus, share fellowship, and thank God.

The Lord's supper as a meal is not a weekly event for me though it is fairly common. In my small group as well as on other occasions, I have led or participated in the Lord's supper as a group meal. The whole meal is a supper that belongs to the Lord.

Why do this? The Lord's supper is a *supper*, that is, it is an evening meal (*deipnon*). Also, I think the supper was intended for smaller groups. The Jerusalem church met to "break bread" in their homes. In addition, the supper as a group meal engenders intimacy among its participants as a sweet moment of fellowship in the Spirit. As we eat together, we commune, show hospitality, and experience grace.

When I lead the Lord's meal, I have a fairly general outline of how it will proceed. While this is not rigid, I think ritual is important or else the meal will lose focus and degenerate into a generality that cannot carry the weight of the moment. While occasions may vary in sequence, Scripture texts, and meditations, below is the general order in which I conduct such meals. (By the way, the food is already on the table when we sit down.) Again, this is suggestive rather than prescriptive.

1. We light candles as a moment of reflection on the meaning of the meal. I light two central candles on the table to symbolize creation and new creation. We give honor and praise to the Father and Son in this way as we remember that the Holy Spirit's flames of love illuminate us and bring us into the presence of the Father and Son. We remember as well that as we eat the bread and drink the wine of the old creation we gather around this table to taste new creation by the power of the Spirit. After the lighting, a brief prayer of thanksgiving is offered.

2. Everyone has a small candle in front of his or her plate. After a thanksgiving prayer, I ask each, in turn, to light their candle and give thanks for something that God is doing in their lives. Thus, our meal begins with our basic response to the light of God's creation and new creation, that is, we give thanks. Gratitude is our fundamental response to what God has done for us.

3. *Someone offers a meditation on the Lord's supper from Scripture.* After these thanksgivings we focus on God's word. The text may be a traditional one like 1 Corinthians 11 or Luke 22. But I don't limit myself to them. Other texts also come into play, such as psalms of thanksgiving (such as Psalms 66, 107, 116, 118). In fact, I will sometimes use a psalm of thanksgiving to begin the whole meal. Other texts can also carry the meaning of the meal, ranging from Israel's Passover and thanksgiving meals to the meals of Jesus during his ministry. Practically, any text that proclaims the gospel, offers thanksgiving, or anticipates the new creation (including the future Messianic banquet) can illuminate the meaning of the table.

4. *Someone breaks the bread of the table.* I recommend a whole loaf that is large enough for every person at the table to take a substantial piece. This bread is also the bread of the meal itself and we continue to eat it throughout. I take the bread in my hands and talk about the meaning of bread. Bread is from the earth and nourishes our bodies; it is part of our daily gift from God. But this bread is also a sacrament of new creation. Through this bread we are nourished by the raised, living body of Christ. We eat this bread for both physical and spiritual nourishment. I then break the bread, offer a prayer of thanksgiving, and distribute it. I give it to the people on either side of me and they break off a piece and pass it down to those

around the table. As each one gives the bread to the other, I encourage them to speak to each other: "This is the body of Christ which is given for you." We all eat from the same loaf, the one body of Christ.

5. We begin eating and drinking what is available on the table. As we continue to eat the bread, we also begin eating the food available on the table. Water is available for everyone. Our conversation is interactive and natural. We talk about our lives, our children, our hopes, and our dreams. We enjoy a meal together in the presence of the risen Lord.

6. We recognize Christ's presence and remember God's work in our lives. At some point near the beginning of the meal, I remind everyone of the two candles and that by the presence of the Spirit, the living Christ is the host of this table. If we have some ongoing intimacy as a group (like an ongoing small group), I will ask each to share something that is happening in their walk with God (struggles, triumphs, hopes). If this group is new or ad hoc, I will ask each to share something about their faith story.

7. We remember the witnesses to faith. Towards the middle of the meal, I will remind us of the communion of the saints. This not only includes the saints around that table and scattered throughout the world but also our communion with the saints who now inhabit the heavens with God. I begin by recalling the presence of Sheila (my deceased wife), Dad, and Joshua (my son who died at the age of sixteen) among others at the table with us, and ask each to remember someone who is already in the heavenlies but present at the table with us. We each speak a name as we go around the table. On occasion we might take the time to share with others why that name is important and how that person nurtured them. In essence, we remember that at the table we commune with the saints as well as with God.

8. *We then have a time of intercession.* I ask each to share a name for which we might pray. Depending on time, we may explain why we named the one we did, but usually we simply speak the name. After each name, we say together, "Lord, hear our prayer." Sometimes someone might lead a prayer for all. I don't usually list the names again in the prayer but simply acknowledge that God has heard us and call God to act. When God's people gather and talk with one another, God listens and remembers (Mal. 3:16).

9. *Someone reads another Scripture.* In this context, I ask another to share a scripture. One of my favorites at this point is Psalm 116. This thanksgiving psalm reminds us that we cannot repay God's goodness except to lift up the cup of thanksgiving and celebrate a meal with God. (The psalm was written in the context of a thanksgiving meal.)

10. *Someone explains the meaning of the cup.* Towards the end of the meal, I take the pitcher that is filled with the fruit of the vine and talk about the "cup" we are about to drink. I remind us that this is the blood of Christ that is poured out for us for the forgiveness of our sins. As we drink we are assured of God's forgiveness—we are reconciled to God and each other. But I also remind us that the cup is something we share with Christ, that is, we share the cup of suffering as persons who follow Jesus to the cross. We are reminded that we are disciples committed to follow Jesus daily, even to a cross.

11. Someone pours the cup. I take the pitcher and pour some into a cup (something like a wine glass perhaps) for the person sitting next to me. As I pour, I say, "This is the blood of Christ for you." In turn, they pour the cup for the person next to them and around the table till all the cups are filled. Someone then prays over the cup, giving thanks for what God has done in Jesus. Then we drink together as we say "Thank you, Father and Lord Jesus."

12. We affirm each other. As we continue to drink from the cup, I ask that everyone speak a word of affirmation to the person for whom they have just poured the cup. In what way do they see Jesus in this person? For what do they give thanks? In this way, we share an intimacy with each other and express our gratitude for each other as we express our gratitude to God.

13. We conclude the meal. As we conclude the meal, I don't want the cup to simply end with a sip. Rather, as we drink and continue to drink (and finish eating as the case may be), I ask each person in turn to share one word (with an explanation) that is most prominent in his or her heart at that moment. What are they experiencing? This is another moment of intimacy in the meal.

14. *We conclude with a benediction.* As the meal winds down and we finish eating, I end the meal with some kind of benediction. It may be a prayer, a blessing, or a Scripture reading. Often, we sing the doxology as a conclusion.

This is a method; it is certainly not a prescriptive standard or *the* method. I expect it to be adapted, changed, and contextualized for diverse settings. The meal can be conducted in any number of ways. There are, however, several things that are, in my opinion, particularly significant. These ground the table in the Word and accentuate the fuller meaning of the supper as an experience of communion and grace that transcends time and space. They are:

+ Soaking the meal in the Word of God.
+ Eating and drinking the body and blood of the Lord.
+ Recognizing the presence of Christ at the table.
+ Communing with the saints across time and space.
+ Interceding for the saints across the world.
+ Expressing gratitude for what God has done for us in Christ.
+ Closing the meal with a benediction.

In this way we embody the table of Jesus as it was experienced in Israel's Passover, in the ministry of Jesus, and at the table of the early church, and we anticipate the coming Messianic banquet.

Conclusion

What does the Lord's supper mean to you? What single word or phrase would best describe your experience of the supper? I have heard a range of answers from "boring" to "contemplative." Whatever our "word" it arises from both our theology and our practice. Without theology, our practice is meaningless. Without practices that embody the theology, we experience a dissonance. In either case the supper becomes irrelevant, unnecessary, and distant.

Renewed practice needs a renewed theological vision, and renewed theology needs practice in order to fully experience what God gives. The Lord's supper is the story of God put into practice, and through that practice God gives Christ to us in a concrete way. The Lord's supper is the gospel in bread and wine. When we eat and drink, God loves us in Christ, communes with as reconciled people, and pours hope into our hearts. Our response, then, is not self-loathing guilt, sadness, or inner turmoil, but gratitude, trusting acceptance of God's grace, and deep joy. That is the table of the Lord within God's new creation.

NEW HEAVEN AND NEW EARTH (Revelation 21-22)

The sea became no more. The waters disappeared. Now, there is no more chaos; there is no more judgment. Death is gone. Tears have been wiped away. Lament has ceased. Pain no longer exists. The waters no longer threaten humanity. There is no more darkness. There is no more curse. The baptism of suffering is *fini*!

"It is done!" Everything has been made new. Heaven and earth, rather than annihilated, have been cleansed by God's holy fire. *They were baptized in a refining fire.* Every evil, every injustice, idolatry, and immorality, has been thrown into the "lake that burns with fire and sulfur." All that remains is God's new pure creation.

A cosmic exodus has taken place. The earth, once filled with suffering, evil, and pain, is now free. The earth, once filled with lament and mourning, is redeemed. The earth has become the inheritance of God's people. Just as Israel went through the waters and wilderness to enter the promised land, so the church has been through the waters and wilderness to receive its inheritance. Together Jews and Gentiles, as the one people of God, inherit the kingdom of God; they inherit the cosmos. The meek now inherit the earth, a new heaven and new earth.

Like the slaughtered Lamb, the people of God have been baptized in suffering just as the heavens and earth have been baptized in fire. Like the resurrected Lamb, the people of God have been raised from their infernal graves to inhabit a new creation that has emerged from the refining fires of the apocalypse.

This new creation, like the original version, is inhabited. There is still a garden but a city has grown up around it. This is not a simple restoration but a transfiguration of the original creation. The whole earth has become a new Jerusalem in which the people of God dwell. The whole earth is a holy city; the whole earth is "holy to the Lord." The glory of the Lord fills the earth as God makes a home among human beings upon the new earth. Heaven and earth have become one, and God dwells with humanity just as in the beginning. There is no temple in this new Jerusalem because the whole city is the temple of God. Indeed, the city is a perfect cube, just like the Holy of Holies in Solomon's temple. The whole earth is now the sanctuary of God, the Holy of Holies.

Sacramental life is now fully renewed. Eden has again appeared on earth. The new earth, emerging out of the sacramental fire of destruction, is renewed with living-giving food and drink. Just as a river flowed out of the heart of Eden, so in the new Jerusalem a river flows from the throne of God and of the Lamb. It is the "water of life." It waters the new earth as it provides drink for those who will never thirst again. The tree of life on either side of the river bears monthly fruit throughout the year, and its leaves are a balm for the nations. The tree gives life just as the water does. Food and drink, like in Eden, are part of God's new creation. *Food and drink are, once again, fully eucharistic!*

All of life is sacramental. The waters of the earth flow from the throne of God and the river waters the fruit trees. Water no longer threatens but gives life. There is no distance between God and humanity. Humanity serves God face to face. God and humanity dwell together in the new creation; their intimacy is renewed. Everything within the new creation rejoices in God and bears the name of God. Even the pots and the pans of the new Jerusalem are inscribed with "Holy to the Lord."

In the new Jerusalem, upon the new heaven and new earth, God will commune with humanity at the messianic banquet table. God will serve the richest food and the finest wines. There the people of God will rejoice with music and dancing.

Cleansed, purified, and washed, we hope to see each other . . . even now when we assemble . . . and in the new heaven and new earth. We hope to eat and drink with each other . . . even now when we assemble . . . and in the new heaven and new earth.

Endnotes

Introduction

[1] John Mark Hicks, Johnny Melton, and Bobby Valentine, *A Gathered People* (Abilene: Leafwood Publishers, 2007).

Chapter 1

[1] Peter Enns, *Exodus*, NIV Application Commentary (Grand Rapids: Zondervan, 2000), 33.

[2] Based on E. P. Sanders, *Judaism: Practice and Belief, 63 BCE-66 CE* (Philadelphia: Trinity Press International, 1992), 110-116.

[3] Terence E. Fretheim, *Exodus*, Interpretation (Louisville: John Knox Press, 1991), 264.

Chapter 2

[1] Kilian McDonnell, "Jesus' Baptism in the Jordan," *Theological Studies* 56 (1995): 210.

Chapter 3

[1] Joel B. Green, "From 'John's Baptism' to 'Baptism in the Name of the Lord Jesus': The Significance of Baptism in Luke-Acts," in *Baptism, the New Testament and the Church: Historical and Contemporary Studies in Honour of R. E. O. White*, JSNTSup 171, ed. Stanley E. Porter and Anthony R. Cross (Sheffield: Sheffield Academic Press, 1999), 161.

[2] Ibid. (Italics are his.)

Chapter 4

[1] N. T. Wright, "The Letter to the Romans," in *The New Interpreter's Bible: A Commentary in Twelve Volumes*, ed. Leander E. Keck (Nashville: Abingdon Press, 2002), 395-770, and *Paul and the Faithfulness of God* (Minneapolis: Fortress Press, 2013), 995-1026.

Chapter 5

[1] Geoffrey Wainwright, *Eucharist and Eschatology* (London: Epworth Press, 1971), 38.

[2] T. F. Torrance, "Eschatology and Eucharist," *Intercommunion*, ed. Donald Baillie and John Marsh (NY: Harper & Brothers, Publishers, 1952), 334.

[3] Rebecca Kuiken, "Hopeful Feasting: Eucharist and Eschatology," in *Hope for Your Future: Theological Voices from the Pastorate*, ed. William H. Lazareth (Grand Rapids: Eerdmans, 2002), 197.

Chapter 6

[1] Accessed November 14, 2013. http://www.oikoumene.org/en/resources/documents/wcc-commissions/faith-and-order-commission/i-unity-the-church-and-its-mission/baptism-eucharist-and-ministry-faith-and-order-paper-no-111-the-lima-text?set_language=en

[2] See Stanley Fowler, "Baptists and Churches of Christ in Search of a Common Theology of Baptism," in *Baptist Sacramentalism* 2, ed. by Anthony R. Cross and Philip E. Thompson (Carlisle: Paternoster, 2008), 254-69 and Brandon C. Jones, "Baptist Sacramental Theology: A Covenantal Framework for Believer Baptism" (PhD dissertation, Calvin Theological Seminary, 2010).

[3] Robert H. Stein, "Baptism and Becoming a Christian in the New Testament," *Southern Baptist Journal of Theology* 2.1 (1998), 6-17.

[4] H. Wayne House, "An Evangelical Response to Baird and Weatherly," in *Evangelicalism and the Stone-Campbell Movement*, ed. William Baker (Grand Rapids: InterVarsity, 2003), 188.

[5] Stein, "Baptism in Luke-Acts," in *Believer's Baptism: Sign of the New Covenant in Christ*, ed. Thomas R. Schreiner and Shawn D. Wright (Nashville: Broadman & Holmann Academic, 2006), 63.

[6] Ibid., 51, and Thomas R. Schreiner, "Baptism in the Epistles," in *Believer's Baptism*, 75.

[7] A. B. Caneday, "Baptism in the Stone-Campbell Restoration Movement," in *Believer's Baptism*, 313.

[8] Ibid., 317.

[9] James W. McClendon, Jr., *Systematic Theology II: Doctrine* (Nashville: Abingdon Press, 1994), 388-389.

[10] Wayne Grudem, *Systematic Theology* (Grand Rapids: Zondervan, 1994), 953-954 (italics in original).

[11] Caneday, "Baptism in the Stone-Campbell," 324-325; cf. 312.

[12] Calvin, *Commentary upon the Acts of the Apostles* (Grand Rapids: Eerdmans, reprint 1949), 1:118.

[13] Alexander Campbell, "Any Christians among the Protestant Parties," *Millennial Harbinger* 8 (September 1837), 412.

[14] Alexander Campbell, *The Campbell-Rice Debate* (Lexington, KY: A. T. Skillman & Son, 1844), 519-20

[15] Alexander Campbell, "Mr. Meredith on Remission," *Millennial Harbinger* 11 (December 1840) 545.

[16] Alexander Campbell, "Any Christians among the Sects?" *Millennial Harbinger* 8 (December 1837) 565.

[17] Campbell, "Christians among the Protestant Parties," 412

[18] James W. McClendon, Jr., *Systematic Theology II: Doctrine* (Nashville: Abingdon, 1994), 396.

Chapter 7

[1] Accessed November 14, 2013. http://www.oikoumene.org/en/resources/documents/wcc-commissions/faith-and-order-commission/i-unity-the-church-and-its-mission/baptism-eucharist-and-ministry-faith-and-order-paper-no-111-the-lima-text?set_language=en

ALSO BY JOHN MARK HICKS

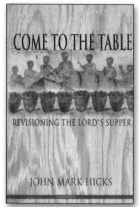

COME TO THE TABLE
Revisioning the Lord's Supper

BY JOHN MARK HICKS

"This is a wonderful, comprehensive, and engaging invitation to deeper understanding of and participation in the Lord's Supper. This will be a most useful book for pastors and congregations."
—**William Willimon**, author of *Sunday Dinner: The Lord's Supper and the Christian Life*

$12.95 205 pages, paper | ISBN 0-9714289-7-2

DOWN IN THE RIVER TO PRAY
Revisioning Baptism as God's Transforming Power

BY JOHN MARK HICKS & GREG TAYLOR

"Hicks and Taylor draw a compelling picture of our baptismal identity and call us into a spirituality shaped by baptismal waters."
—**Robert Webber**, author of *Ancient-Future Faith*

$14.99 282 pages, paper | ISBN 0-9728425-3-5
Teacher Resource DVD available, $34.95

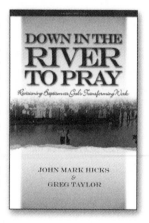

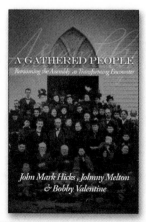

A GATHERED PEOPLE
Revisioning the Assembly as Transforming Encounter

JOHN MARK HICKS, JOHNNY MELTON & BOBBY VALENTINE

An in depth biblical, historical, and theological study of the Christian assembly or Lord's day, concluding with reflections on Christian assemblies today.

$14.99, 224 pages | ISBN 978-0-89112-550-1

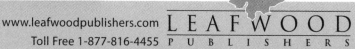

www.leafwoodpublishers.com
Toll Free 1-877-816-4455

LEAFWOOD PUBLISHERS